PLAY NICE IN YOUR SANDBOX AT CHURCH

Endorsements

"I always enjoy reading manuscripts, and it was my pleasure to read Ron Price's manuscript for his new book *Play Nice in Your Sandbox at Church*. Ron did a great job in presenting some practical applications with just the right amount of humor and some common sense ways to be a better church member. I hope you enjoy the book as much as I have. Some of the stories you will remember forever. The book intends to develop, maintain, and enhance relationships. With that prayer, I hope that you will use some of the nuggets in Ron's book to 'play nice'."

Dr. Joseph L. Bunce Executive Director,
Baptist Convention of New Mexico

"For years, when washing the dishes each night, I would be able to watch our kids play in our sandbox with all the neighbor kids. Inevitably, one of the neighbor boys would start throwing sand, grab his Tonka truck, and go home. Having been a pastor for 35 years, I know that things are not very different in the church today. In this book, Ron draws upon years of ministry experience, a good dose of scripture, and riveting stories to provide practical instruction in how to prevent and deal with conflict in the church today. I would recommend the book to anyone interested in playing well in the 'sandbox' called the church."

Steve Sonderman, Executive Director of No Regrets Men's Ministry

"Conflicts are inevitable! Ron Price in *Play Nice in Your Sandbox at Church* has provided us with the practical, biblical, and spiritual solutions to unraveling, complicated interpersonal relationships. I encourage you to buy a box of books for you and your team today!"

Dr. James O. Davis Founder/President
Global Church Network Orlando, Florida

"*Play Nice in Your Sandbox* is an informative, insightful, and hard-hitting book written for those who desire a high-quality Church life. Ron Price gives the reader a feeling of personally talking one-on-one while sitting in his living room, taking you on a soul searching journey into a place of understanding what a healthy Church life looks like. You will see that Ron cares deeply about Church life and shares his deepest thoughts on the subject. If you are a Christian who desires warm Church relationships, this book is a home run, and a must-read for you!"

Lemuel Baker, Ph.D. Author of *The Many Faces of Judaism*
- Senior Fellow Lemuel Baker Ministries Center for Learning!

"It is my privilege to oversee one hundred and thirty churches over three different states. We serve right around eighteen thousand members. As I read this book by Ron Price, I thought to myself, it would be nice to buy a copy for every member. Ron has a great sense of humor, and just the right mix of quotes both from the Bible and other writers to make the book interesting and enjoyable. He really gets to the bottom of the issues in getting along at church."

Ed Barnett President of the Rocky Mountain Conference
of Seventh-day Adventists.

"*Play Nice in Your Sandbox at Church*, a new book by Ron Price, is a much-needed resource for our times. It is truly valuable for any pastor, church leader, and all who would read its impacting message. The book is excellent in presenting our ever-changing world and the never-changing principles of God's Word to help us through these times. Each of this book's chapters addresses a vital spiritual need of our times with Biblical truth, practical insight, a road for psychological health, a humorous slant, and many unforgettable illustrations.

The issues that the author confronts is done in a loving way with an invitation to deeper spiritual growth for believers. The message of eternal salvation through Jesus Christ, our Lord and Savior, is repeated in the book so that one who is not a believer can come to that personal relationship with Jesus Christ. Every chapter in this book is well documented with many Scripture passages and gives a practical application for a reader to discover. A holy and humble walk with the Lord awaits all who seriously receive this message. The many humorous injections that couple with spiritual wisdom will give any reader a deeper insight into the Christian life as taught and exemplified by Jesus Christ. An invitation to those who have been wounded in church battles, a journey of a deeper faith, a route to greater spiritual wisdom combine to bless all who read the message of *Play Nice in Your Sandbox at Church*."

Dr. Wayne Norton Baptist Minister, Leadership Consultant, and Author of *Norton's Nuggets from the New Testament*

An 8-Step Model to Help You Prevent or Resolve
Conflict With Your Brothers and Sisters

PLAY NICE
IN YOUR SANDBOX
at Church

RON PRICE, MA

NASHVILLE

NEW YORK • LONDON • MELBOURNE • VANCOUVER

Play Nice in Your Sandbox at Church

An 8-Step Model to Help You Prevent or Resolve Conflict with Your Brothers and Sisters

Published in New York, New York, by Morgan James Publishing. Morgan James is a trademark of Morgan James, LLC. www.MorganJamesPublishing.com

ISBN 9781642799859 paperback
ISBN 9781642799866 eBook
Library of Congress Control Number: 2020930255

Cover & Interior Design by:
Christopher Kirk
www.GFSstudio.com

Edited by:
Jennifer Harshman (Harshman Services) and Erica Herra

Unless otherwise noted, all Scripture references are from the HOLY BIBLE, NEW LIVING TRANSLATION (NLT): Scriptures taken from the HOLY BIBLE, NEW LIVING TRANSLATION, Copyright© 1996, 2004, 2007 by Tyndale House Foundation. Used by permission of Tyndale House Publishers, Inc., Carol Stream, Illinois 60188. All rights reserved.
Scriptures marked NIV are taken from the NEW INTERNATIONAL VERSION (NIV): Scripture taken from THE HOLY BIBLE, NEW INTERNATIONAL VERSION ®. Copyright© 1973, 1978, 1984, 2011 by Biblica, Inc.™. Used by permission of Zondervan
Scriptures marked KJV are taken from the KING JAMES VERSION (KJV): KING JAMES VERSION, public domain.

Morgan James is a proud partner of Habitat for Humanity Peninsula and Greater Williamsburg. Partners in building since 2006.

Get involved today! Visit
MorganJamesPublishing.com/giving-back

Dedication

As I strive to do with all aspects of my life,
I dedicate this book to my Lord and Savior Jesus Christ.
While writing, my prayer was always
"Lord You write, I'll type." To Him be the Glory!

I would be remiss if I did not also mention my wife Maridell,
with whom I have shared 38 wonderful years of marriage –
and two that were not so good. Ok, a bad joke,
but I do appreciate her sticking by me all these years through,
as they say, "thick and thin."

Table of Contents

Acknowledgments

First and foremost, I thank my Lord and Savior Jesus Christ for inspiring and enabling me to write this book. It's been quite a journey, but joyful for the vast majority.

I also want to thank the numerous contributors who, for various reasons, shall remain unidentified. In preparation for writing, I solicited stories from people of times when God's people have not acted in a Godlike fashion. What's that expression "Be careful what you ask for?" Suffice to say; I received plenty, from clergy and laity alike, more than I could use, in fact.

As some of those scenarios were sensitive, I chose to make them as unrecognizable as possible. Thus, the omission of names and the altering of certain details. Hopefully you who contributed know that I am both sorry for what you had to share, but grateful for your willingness to help. Let's hope, and pray, that others will learn from your stories and not have to experience them themselves.

As with any project, you encounter financial costs along the way. I especially thank Shirley Stewart, Wes Stewart, and Barbara and Larry Van

Ryan for believing in me and backing up their belief with much needed and appreciated funds.

Much of this book was written in the comfort of the Best Western Plus Four Corners Inn. Donele Fowler and her excellent staff provided everything I needed to help get this book done, and I am grateful.

Working with Morgan James Publishing has been a wonderful experience. You would have to search far and wide to find a more competent and helpful partner. From the beginning, they helped me feel like a member of their family. I cannot find the words to tell you how grateful I am for their numerous contributions to this book.

You will likely find few if any grammatical mistakes in this book. The credit for that goes to Jennifer Harshman and Erica Herra for their excellent editing, which I appreciate so much.

And, lastly, there have been so many people God has placed in my life to help me see Him more clearly. I would so like to express my appreciation to each one by name, but that would likely double the size of this book. Suffice to say I am truly grateful, and please know I could not have written this book without your wisdom, help, and support.

Introduction

I have often said that the title *PLAY NICE in Your Sandbox at Church* has to be among the dumbest titles you have ever heard. Do we really need a book that tells Christians they ought to get along with each other? Well, obviously, since you are holding this book in your hands, I felt the need existed and that it was my duty/privilege to attempt to meet that need.

The sandbox is an appropriate metaphor for life and how we should all strive to get along with each other. Unfortunately, we grow up, and that getting along business gets more challenging. And, while the sandbox is often a place for fun and happiness, it can also get messy at times. That sounds like church to me—how about you?

As you will soon discover, the PLAY and NICE are capitalized because they are acronyms. PLAY represents a four-step model to prevent conflict when possible, and NICE gives a four-step model to resolve differences with others.

I must warn you that this book is grounded in Scripture as well as conflict resolution theory. If you do not accept that the Bible is the absolute Word of God, this book may not be for you (see 2 Timothy 3:16–17). I do not claim to be a theologian, clergyperson, or seminary graduate, but I am in my 41st year of walking with the Lord and seeking to know His Word and His will. For 30 of those 41 years, I have worked as a mediator/arbitrator, helping people resolve a wide range of disputes. I have also been fortunate to attend numerous conferences and workshops, honing my skill in alternative dispute resolution. Drawing from that experience and training, in 2016, I wrote *PLAY NICE in Your Sandbox at Work.*

After I earned my Masters Degree in Counseling in 1994, I added marriage and relationship coaching to my private practice. As an admitted training enthusiast, some might say "junkie", I attended several Smart-Marriage conferences, from which I gained valuable knowledge about marriage—what makes it work and what causes it to fail. That education led me in 2003 to cofound the Four Corners Coalition for Marriage & Family. It also contributed mightily to my second book, *PLAY NICE in Your Sandbox at Home*, which came out in 2018.

I tell you all this to make the point that I have put myself in the midst of conflict for the majority of my adult life. If that doesn't tell you I'm a sick man, I don't know what will, but I am grateful for the knowledge I have acquired over the years. It is my privilege and joy to share that knowledge with you. Be sure to check out the Bonus/Call to Action page at the end of this book for details on how you can enroll in a free mini course on Relationship CPR (Conflict Prevention & Resolution).

Conflict is not new for the human race. The very first conflict we know of in human history occurred between two sons of our species' first parents. In Genesis chapter four, we read the story of Cain and Abel. *Spoiler alert:* It does not end well.

Conflict and disagreements in the church are nothing new, either. In Acts 15, we read of a rift between two of God's greatest evangelists, Paul and Barnabus. Their dispute was so severe that they split up, with each taking a new partner to continue their work. In retrospect, while it might have been nicer for them to split up on peaceful terms, their parting likely multiplied their overall effectiveness.

Read Acts 6:1, when the new church was rapidly growing, "there were rumblings of discontent." Hopefully, I've made the case that conflict between people, even God's people in His Church, has been around for a long, long time. My friend Pastor Keith Berryman compares churches to the human autoimmune system, which at times malfunctions and causes severe problems by fighting against itself. I think he's onto something there.

Face it. We are all imperfect human beings, and to think there will never be misunderstandings or disagreements among imperfect people is foolhardy. As you will read in this book, and in my previous two books in the series (not-so-subtle hint ☺), conflict between people is inevitable in any setting. It is also true that conflict need not always result in a negative outcome. But, oh my, it sure can get to be that way when not handled well.

Throughout this book, you will find numerous Scriptures that address conflict within a church and which detail how God wants His children to get along. You should not be surprised that whatever God wants for His children, our common enemy, known as satan (his name does not deserve to be capitalized), the devil, or the adversary, wants the exact opposite. In John 10:10, we read, "The thief's purpose is to steal and kill and destroy. My purpose (Jesus said) is to give them a rich and satisfying life." You must admit that both have accomplished their purposes over the ages. You must also realize that neither has yet conceded or given up in the epic battle for the souls of humankind. Jesus warned us that we must stick together in the struggle for "A kingdom divided by civil war will collapse" (Mark 3:25).

If the Church is to be victorious, it is essential that God's people get along, or play nice in their sandbox, if you will. We truly do need each other. The English poet, author, and humorist Thomas Hood posed the question, "When was ever honey made with one bee in a hive?" And, as Paul wrote so eloquently in Romans 12:4–5: "Just as our bodies have many parts and each part has a special function, so it is with Christ's body. We are many parts of one body, and we all belong to each other." He continues in verse 18, "Do all you can to live in peace with everyone."

In another passage, Paul gives evidence that he was greatly distressed by conflict among believers, especially perhaps among members of churches he helped to plant. Look at what he wrote in 1 Corinthians 1:10: "I appeal to you, dear brothers and sisters, by the authority of our Lord Jesus Christ, to live in harmony with each other. Let there be no divisions in the church. Rather, be of one mind, united in thought and purpose."

If God's people would live by that verse alone, we would have so much more peace, joy, and happiness. If that were the case, I would never have even thought about writing this book.

My goal in writing this book is not that we will all become perfect Christians and attend churches where never is heard a discouraging word, and the skies are not cloudy all day (Younger readers may want to listen to the "Home on the Range" song to understand my wording). In Psalm 55:12–14, King David penned some very disheartening words: "It is not an enemy who taunts me—I could bear that. It is not my foes who so arrogantly insult me—I could have hidden from them. Instead, it is you—my equal, my companion and close friend. What good fellowship we once enjoyed as we walked together to the house of God."

It is my fervent hope that God will use this book to help His children to pause before taking offense and thereby preventing a conflict with a fellow believer, or that they will follow His direction to resolve differences before they have the chance to escalate and cause wide-spread damage.

I divided this book into two major portions covering eight sections. The first four sections comprise the PLAY chapters, which are designed to help you prevent needless trivial matters from escalating into situations you neither want nor need. Sections five through eight entail the NICE portion of the book, in which you will learn specific tools, tips, and techniques with which to resolve significant differences you are bound to have with others from time to time.

You will find a CHAPTER CHALLENGE at the end of each chapter. If you are at all like me, it is too easy to learn new information but not have it impact your life. In these challenges, I sought to give you some ideas through which you might implement the information you read. I'm confident you will come up with some suggestions of your own, and I would love to hear about them if you care to share. For that purpose or any other concern you might have please feel free to reach out to me at *Ron@PlayNiceinYourSandbox.com*

So, I thank you for reading this book, and I wholeheartedly thank God for permitting me to be His instrument to get it to you. As I wrote it, my prayer was always, "Lord, You write; I'll type."

One last note. This is your book, and you may read it however you like. I did not write it to be read cover to cover, but rather one chapter or section at a time. Please consider focusing on just one tool, tip, or technique to practice for a week, then continue to practice that one and add just one more. In week three, continue to focus on the first two and add one more. For all subsequent weeks, drop your focus on the earliest and add one more so you are focusing on no more than three at any time.

Research on forming habits varies. I've seen estimates that it takes between 21 and 60 days to incorporate a new pattern into your life.

There is also research that shows if you try to make four or more changes at one time, you are not likely to accomplish any with success. Three seems to be the most we humans can handle at one time.

Okay, one more final word. This book contains lots of common sense and is intended for those of us who have the ability to practice common sense. Intending no malice toward any, it is a well established fact that we daily walk among people who for various and often unknown reasons do not operate from a socially accepted and defined set of principles. If you are in a situation where you are being harassed, threatened, or in any way made to feel unsafe around a fellow church member, please, by all means, take precautionary steps to protect yourself and your loved ones. I'm convinced that the concepts you are about to read in this book will help you to prevent insignificant situations from escalating to full-blown conflict, and you will also be better equipped to address conflict that has already taken root and needs to be addressed. But despite the risk of repeating myself, this applies when you are dealing with someone who chooses to cooperate with your efforts and is able to do so.

Also, please note there may be times when you should seek neutral or perhaps professional help if a situation has already gotten out of hand or to prevent one from doing so. There may be some situations where the parties are too hurt to be able to deal directly with each other. There is, or should be, no shame in reaching out for assistance in such cases. In every case, please keep in mind the counsel found in Hebrews 4:15–16: "This High Priest of ours understands our weaknesses, for he faced all of the same testings we do, yet he did not sin. So let us come boldly to the throne of our gracious God. There we will receive his mercy, and we will find grace to help us when we need it most."

Section One:
PRAY, PRAY, PRAY

Key text: Philippians 4:4–7: "Always be full of joy in the Lord. I say it again—rejoice! Let everyone see that you are considerate in all you do. Remember, the Lord is coming soon. Don't worry about anything; instead, pray about everything. Tell God what you need, and thank him for all he has done. Then you will experience God's peace, which exceeds anything we can understand. His peace will guard your hearts and minds as you live in Christ Jesus."

Quote: *"Prayer is not preparation for the work—prayer is the work."*
—Oswald Chambers

*L*ife is hard. Okay, that's not exactly a newsflash, but isn't it also true that often we make it harder than it needs to be? Numerous times in Scripture, we are admonished to pray, to reach out and connect with our Heavenly Father. He is usually much more willing to give us aid and comfort than we are to ask Him. This is certainly true when we find ourselves embroiled in conflict with someone. One of my most often used expressions is "Conflict is inevitable; damaged relationships are optional."

As human beings, we will find ourselves in conflict with others at times. That's just a result of our human nature, and, by the way, have you ever noticed that whenever we use the term "human nature," we are never describing something positive and admirable?

Conflict in the world is certainly understandable where life is based on a "dog eat dog" philosophy and mindset. But conflict in the church? Conflict between individuals who claim to be followers of the same Lord—how do you explain that? My simple explanation is that at those times, we have forgotten who we are, who they are, and, most importantly, *Whose* we all are. While all situations are unique in themselves, I can just about guarantee you that if you find yourself in conflict with a church member, or another Christian, your focus is more on yourself or on them than it is on God.

The Christian Church does not lack for information on various forms of prayer. Some of my personal favorites are conversational prayer in groups, praying the Lord's Prayer, intercessory prayer, the ACTS Prayer (Adoration, Confession, Thanksgiving, Supplication), praying with Bible promises, or simply while reading passages of Scripture. I heard of one little girl who prayed the alphabet out loud. When asked why she did this, she replied, "If I give God the letters, He'll put them into words for me." My purpose in writing this book—and I hope God's purpose in having me write it—is not so much to teach you how to pray as to encourage that you do more of it, especially when you are trying to keep the peace and prevent conflict.

When someone does something that offends you, you have two immediate choices. You can either react to the offense, or you can respond to it in a Christlike manner. Choose the first option, and you can expect the situation to get worse—perhaps much worse than it needs to be.

Choose the second option, and prepare to be astounded by how God works in both of your lives and the situation.

I wrote in *PLAY NICE in Your Sandbox at Work* that hurting people are going to hurt people. They don't have to plan their attack or devise elaborate schemes. When someone is hurting, they will, by nature, reach out and hurt someone else. So, if someone has just hurt or offended you, I challenge you to focus more on how you might ease their pain than on how their actions made you feel. I realize that may not always be easy to do based on the severity of the offense, but I can guarantee you it is what Christ would have you do as one of His followers. He may want to use you to help heal another of His children, but if you take offense and seek to retaliate, you and He will lose that opportunity.

Prayer in a conflict situation changes everything. Maybe not right away, and perhaps you won't feel any different, but as my friend Jasper Welch says, "TTP—Trust the Process." When you genuinely invite God to intervene in your life and your situation, He will do so. Remember the words written to us in James 1:5: "If you need wisdom, ask our generous God, and He will give it to you. He will not rebuke you for asking."

It is difficult to stay angry or upset with someone for whom you are earnestly praying and seeking God's blessing. Again, you may or may not feel differently after you pray for the other person or the situation, but your feelings are not what matters. Seeking and implementing God's plan and purpose for you should be your highest priority. We read in Mathew 5:43–45 "You have heard the law that says 'Love your neighbor' and hate your enemy. But I (Jesus) say love your enemies! Pray for those who persecute you. In that way, you will be acting as true children of your Father in Heaven. For He gives His sunlight to both the evil and the good, and He sends rain on the just and the unjust alike."

In one of the most well-known portions of Scripture, Jesus disciples came to Him with an urgent request: "Lord, teach us to pray, just as John taught his disciples." Many feel their request was that Jesus would teach them *how* to pray, and as we read in Luke 11:1–4, He did precisely that. But I believe their desire could also have been exactly as the wording says, that He would teach them to remain in a continuous state of dependence upon God as He did; that they would make prayer a frequent and regular component of their lives, not only at meals and at times of urgent need. Jesus goes on in Luke 11 to instruct His followers that they should pray repeatedly, not just once and done. As you pray for wisdom, also pray for added grace, love, compassion, and understanding. Whatever you pray for yourself, consider praying a double portion for the other person(s) (see 1 Timothy 2:1 NLT).

In the heat of the moment, or when you don't know what to pray, you can always use the eight-word prayer, which I first heard from evangelist Mike Flynn: "O God, O God, O God, O God!"

Why do we pray? Why does God encourage us so often in Scripture to pray? What does it mean to "pray without ceasing?" (1 Th 5:17). Is it to get Him to do as we desire? I certainly hope not! Prayer is our connection with God. Just as communication is vital to the health of any human relationship, even more so, it is essential for a healthy relationship with God. Seek to maintain an attitude of prayer, of connection, of dependence, of gratitude. Jesus, our best example for every aspect of life, spent many entire nights in prayer.

CHAPTER CHALLENGE: Follow the Biblical counsel found in 1 Th 5:16–18: "Always be joyful. Never stop praying. Be thankful in all circumstances, for this is God's will for you who belong to Christ Jesus." The next time you find yourself at odds with someone, ask God what He would have you do. As the world-famous "Author Unknown" said, "Prayer should be a first step, not a last resort." Seek His counsel before you resort to your own will. Remember that conflict holds great potential for bringing about God's purposes, and be ever willing to cooperate with His plan (see Section Eight).

CHAPTER P1:

Praise Ye the Lord!

Key text: 1 Thessalonians 5:16–18: "Always be joyful. Never stop praying. Be thankful in all circumstances, for this is God's will for you who belong to Christ Jesus."

Quote: *"Praise should be an integral part of prayer life. The more you praise God, the less time you'll have to quarrel or find fault with others."*

—Ron Price

I'm a firm believer in science—at least when what science determines or "discovers" aligns with the Bible. When I am faced with a decision to accept the word of man (science) or the Word of God (The Holy Spirit and the Bible), that's just not even a contest.

Take, for example, the current controversy over "climate change." Now, don't worry, I'm not about to begin a debate on the topic. I personally accept that the climate is changing, much like it has in previous times before even the thought of carbon emissions was present. I do not, however, believe that climate change is man-caused or that man can do much if anything about it. That is in the realm of God's authority, and He will let happen whatever best serves His ultimate purposes. With that in mind, I should also point out our responsibility as Christians to care for the earth, and not to contribute in any way to it's destruction.

An area of science that I do accept and, for the most part, agree with is called the study of positive psychology. One description I found said, "Positive psychology is the scientific study of what makes life most worth living." Another definition said it is "the scientific study of positive human functioning and flourishing on multiple levels that include the biological, personal relational, institutional, cultural, and global dimensions of life." Wow, maybe I should have stopped with "the scientific study of what makes life most worth living"?

Whatever the definition, you can be sure that gratitude and thankfulness are significant components of positive psychology and a successful, satisfying life. Maintaining an attitude of appreciation and gratitude will also help you prevent possible conflicts with church members and others from ever developing. Doing such will help you overlook minor infractions that otherwise might get you embroiled in a full-blown conflict situation.

In positive psychology research, gratitude often correlates highly with happiness—the more grateful you are, the happier you are likely to be. It also correlates highly with overall health and well-being.

Various studies on the impact of gratitude and thankfulness list benefits such as:

Improved physical health;

Improved psychological health;

Improved sleep (which contributes to numerous side benefits);

Improved relationships with the significant people in your life;

Improved self-esteem; and on and on and on . . .

In the process of preparing to write this chapter, I came across numerous quotes dealing with the subject. Tecumseh, a Shawnee warrior, and chief in the late 18th and early 19th centuries said, "When you rise in the morning, give thanks for the light, for your life, for your strength. Give thanks for your food, and for the joy of living. If you see no reason to give thanks, the fault lies in yourself."

Author Sam Lefkowitz relates: "When asked if my cup is half full or half empty my only response is that I am thankful that I have a cup."

And, lastly, "Gratitude shouldn't be an occasional incident, but a continuous attitude," so says businessman, author, and syndicated columnist Harvey Mackay.

Now, lest you think this is solely a secular topic, here are just a few of several verses I found in God's Word:

Psalm 92 1–2 says, "It is good to give thanks to the LORD, to sing praises to the Most High. It is good to proclaim your unfailing love in the morning, your faithfulness in the evening, accompanied by a ten-stringed instrument, a harp, and the melody of a lyre."

Philippians 4:4–7 reads, "Always be full of joy in the Lord. I say it again—rejoice! Let everyone see that you are considerate in all you do. Remember, the Lord is coming soon. Don't worry about anything; instead, pray about everything. Tell God what you need and thank him for all he has done. Then you will experience God's peace, which exceeds anything we can understand. His peace will guard your hearts and minds as you live in Christ Jesus."

You'll find a famous verse in Proverbs 17:22: "A cheerful heart is good medicine, but a broken spirit saps a person's strength." Aren't you glad that modern-day science "discovered" this truth that was written for us way back when?

There are so many more texts we could look at that prove beyond a shadow of a doubt that God's ultimate plan is that you be aware of His many blessings. Once aware, you can then live out His blessings and share them with others. What would your church be like if more members were doing that?

Mae Duley Ogdon wrote the hymn "Brighten the Corner Where You Are" in the late 1800s. We don't hear that hymn much anymore, not nearly as much as we should. It is wonderful counsel for all people, perhaps especially, dare I say, at church.

William Arthur Ward, an American writer, is quoted as having written, "Feeling gratitude and not expressing it is like wrapping a present and not giving it." Feeling grateful to someone is nice, but please don't stop there—let them know.

While I have never been nor do I ever plan to be a pastor, I have been privileged to do my share of preaching in various churches. Over 30 years ago, I received an anonymous letter from someone in a church where I occasionally spoke thanking me for my preaching and for the blessing he or she received therefrom. Suffice to say, I still have that letter.

In closing, I have two more quotes that I just could not leave out of this chapter:

"Start each day by affirming peaceful, contented, and happy attitudes, and your days will then be pleasant and successful," said Norman Vincent Peale. That sure sounds like wise advice to me!

And, finally, Abe Lincoln said, "Most folks are as happy as they make up their mind to be." Please determine that by God's grace you will be a happy, grateful person.

CHAPTER CHALLENGE: Who can you show gratitude and appreciation to? Decide how you will do so within the next three days.

Search online for "gratitude" or "thankful" quotes and ponder a new one several days each week. Better yet, do a Bible search for the words "grateful" or "thankful" and choose a verse to memorize and repeat often throughout each day.

You've heard the expression that you are what you eat. There is certainly some truth in that statement, but perhaps, even more, you are what you allow into your mind. Consider taking a 30day news fast or at least one day per week to limit the influx of negative thoughts and focus solely on the positive.

CHAPTER P2:

Can Laughter Prevent Conflict?

Key text: Proverbs 17:22: "A cheerful heart is good medicine, but a broken spirit saps a person's strength."

Quote: *"I have not seen anyone dying of laughter, but I know millions who are dying because they are not laughing."*

—Dr. Madan Kataria

An Irish proverb claims, "A good night's sleep and a good hearty laugh will cure most ills." American writer Madeleine L'Engle said, "A good laugh heals a lot of hurts." There is a plethora (I've always liked that word) of research available today about the health benefits of laughter. Among these benefits are lower blood pressure, a stronger immune system, increased creativity, and many, many more.

Norman Cousins, the author of *Anatomy of an Illness,* formed the habit of laughing each night before he went to sleep. He found that on average, ten minutes of deep, hearty laughter gave him two hours of pain-free sleep. He also regained his health after being diagnosed with an incurable and irreversible bone disease. You should not be surprised at these findings, for after all God is the Originator of laughter, and He clearly said it is beneficial for you.

Laughter provides social benefits, for as the Danish comedian Victor Borge said, "The shortest distance between two people is laughter." In some respects, I decided to include this chapter just for fun because I genuinely enjoy God's gift of laughter. Please don't miss the point, however, that laughter can help to break down barriers and prevent conflict. While it is difficult to stay angry with someone you are praying for, the same might be said for someone with whom you share a good laugh.

So just in case you haven't laughed in a while, did you hear about the prayer meeting where one of the senior citizens beseeched God to "rid our lives of the cobwebs of sin." The next week she repeated verbatim her plea that God would "rid our lives of the cobwebs of sin." This scenario went on for week after week, until in exasperation, a fellow member prayed, "O Lord, please kill that spider!"

Perhaps you've seen the bumper sticker that poses the profound philosophical question: "What if the Hokey Pokey really is what it's all about?" There is some doubt as to who should get credit for composing the song, which was popular in the 1950s. On a sad note, I heard that when one of the men believed to have written it died, the morticians had quite the challenge getting him in the casket. Apparently, when they put his left foot in, he put his left foot out . . .

Truth be told, we really need healthy relationships with others to live a satisfied and meaningful life. Zig Ziglar agreed with this assertion, but he also believed we need some alone time now and then. He claimed that was the impetus for the invention of the 23-hour deodorant. He also appreciated the deodorant called "Stereo" which doesn't really hide the odor, but it makes it so others can't tell from where it is coming.

Everyone has a sense of humor, but unfortunately, some have felt they had to stifle theirs for one reason or another. If that is true for you, let me encourage you to rediscover yours. Don't think you have to be a professional comedian or humorist to share your gift with others. As my friend and master punster Jim Baker often says, "Be yourself—everyone else is already taken." He also advises people to "Be nice to everyone you know, for without them, you would be a total stranger."

Humor and sources of laughter are all about you if you take the time to look. Some of my favorites are videos, puns, sharing embarrassing personal moments, humorous bulletin typos, and of course, jokes.

My favorite joke of all time, at least the one I tell most often, involves a poet and a rocket scientist who were seated next to each other on a long train ride. After a while, the rocket scientist said, "I'm bored," and the poet replied, "Me too." The rocket scientist suggested they play a game in which they would each ask the other a question, and if stumped, they must pay the other $5.00.

The poet replied, "A poet against a rocket scientist in a knowledge bowl? I don't think so."

"Okay," the scientist said, "I'll sweeten the deal." He went on to tell the poet that he would ask him a question, and the penalty for not answering correctly would be $5.00. The poet could then ask him a question, for which an incorrect answer would cost $50.00. The poet accepted the terms and invited the rocket scientist to ask the first question.

The rocket scientist replied with, "How far is it from the earth to the sun?" After searching his memory banks and failing to locate the correct answer, the poet handed over a five-dollar bill and said, "Man, you got me. I don't know."

The rocket scientist replied, "Thank you very much, and by the way, it happens to be 92.96 million miles."

For his part, the poet turned to the rocket scientist and asked him, "What animal went up the mountain on three legs and came down on four?" The rocket scientist was beside himself. He had never heard such a question. He searched and searched for an answer, but none came. He took out a fifty-dollar bill and handed it to the poet while saying, "Man, you got me. I don't know," to which the poet replied, "Thank you very much."

Expecting to hear the correct answer, the rocket scientist asked: "Wait a minute, what animal went up the mountain on three legs and came down on four?" at which point the poet took out a five-dollar bill, handed it to the rocket scientist and said, "Man, you got me—I don't know."

And, lastly, did you hear about the pastor who went to visit one of his members. He knew she was home, so he knocked on the door. After knocking a few times and getting no response, the pastor took out his business card and wrote on the back "Revelation 3:20." He stuck the card in the door and walked off in a huff. A bit later, the woman came to the door and found the business card. She went to her Bible and read, "Behold I stand at the door and knock. If anyone will answer, I will come in and sup with them." Well, the next week, the pastor found his business card in the offering plate. Revelation 3:20 had been crossed out and was replaced by Genesis 3:10. The pastor went to his Bible, turned to that verse, and read, "Behold I heard your voice, but I was naked so I hid myself."

I believe it was the American lawyer and scholar Felix Cohen who said, "Generally the theories we believe we call facts, and the facts we disbelieve we call theories." So true! There can, or at least should be, no doubt that it is a fact that laughter does a body good. That goes for an individual's body and a church body as well. But, please do not take my word for it—check it out for yourself. Life is hard, but with some regularly added laughter, you'll find it gets a tad easier. You might also find yourself experiencing less conflict with others.

CHAPTER CHALLENGE: Consider volunteering to serve on your church's social committee. If one is not in place, check with your pastor or church leadership to ask if you can gather some other members together to form one. Do your part to make sure laughter is a regular component of your life and that of your church body.

Commit to spending some time each day in hearty laughter. You won't go wrong if you look up Taylor Mason, Jeff Allen, or Tim Hawkins on YouTube. Each of these gentlemen provides hours of great humor in a clean, God-honoring way.

CHAPTER P3:

Heaven, We Have a Problem

Key text: Mt. 24:11–13: "And many false prophets will appear and will deceive many people. Sin will be rampant everywhere, and the love of many will grow cold. But the one who endures to the end will be saved."

Quote: *"Red Letter Christians believe in the doctrines of the Apostle's Creed, are convinced that the Scriptures have been inspired by the Holy Spirit, and make having a personal transforming relationship with the resurrected Christ the touchstone of their faith."*

—Tony Campolo

I adapted the title for this chapter from Number 50 of the American Film Institution's Top 100 movie quotes of all time. You may have guessed the actual quote to which I refer is "Houston, we have a problem" from the movie Apollo 13. That movie depicted a real-life experience that was fraught with danger and potential catastrophe. As dangerous as that situation was, however, I dare say, "Heaven, we have a problem" is infinitely more severe in its scope and consequences.

In Revelation Chapters 2 and 3, the Apostle John—under the guidance and inspiration of the Holy Spirit—wrote letters from Jesus to various churches in his day. Many believe the churches are symbolic of particular ages of human history. If true, the final message to the Laodicean church must hold relevance for the end of earthly time, a time many believe we are presently in or at least rapidly approaching.

Starting in Chapter 3, verse 15, we read, "I know all the things you do, that you are neither hot nor cold. I wish that you were one of the other! But since you are like lukewarm water, neither hot nor cold, I will spit you out of my mouth. You say, 'I am rich. I have everything I want. I don't need a thing!' And you don't realize that you are wretched and miserable and poor and blind and naked." Am I the only one who thinks this sounds way too much like many modern-day Christians and churches in America?

Heaven, we have a problem, and I, for one, believe we are running out of time to remedy the situation. I propose that at the heart of the problem is our individual and collective disregard of the Holy Spirit in our lives, and that could very well help to explain why so many of God's children get crosswise with each other at times.

Pastor and Author A.W. Tozer contends, "If you were to remove the Holy Spirit from the early church, 95% of what they did would have ceased." He goes on to say, "If you were to remove the Holy Spirit from today's church, 95% of what we do would continue as-is." Ouch!

It is plain from Scripture that God describes two types of His "followers"—Spiritual and Carnal. Please note, I said both are His followers, which means both groups attend church often, perhaps regularly. Let me caution you to be very careful to not judge anyone other than yourself as to which camp a person is in.

Spiritual people, you likely know, are the ones who have the Holy Spirit living in them. In Revelation 3, they are called "hot." In Mathew

5, the parable of the Ten Virgins, they are referred to as "wise." It is interesting to note that all ten were waiting for the Bridegroom, all brought their lamps filled with oil, and all fell asleep. The wise, however, had an abundance of oil, enough to help them do what they needed to do, while the foolish did not have enough in reserve.

Oil in Scripture is often used as a symbol of the Holy Spirit. Spiritual Christians, therefore, are those who have died to self and who rely on the indwelling Holy Spirit to guide them, to comfort them, and to equip them for the battles of life. Carnal Christians, on the other hand, hold back from total surrender and dependence upon Christ. They try to do life their way, and far too often rely on their own efforts, futile though they are.

Perhaps the most explicit definition of Spiritual vs. Carnal Christians is found in Galatians 5:16–17, where we read: "So I say, let the Holy Spirit guide your lives. Then you won't be doing what your sinful nature craves. The sinful (or Carnal) nature wants to do evil, which is just the opposite of what the Spirit wants. And the Spirit gives us desires that are opposite of what the sinful nature desires. These two forces are constantly fighting each other, so you are not free to carry out your good intentions."

Please remember my purpose in writing this book; I hope God's purpose in prompting me to write it is to draw attention to the fact that conflict among God's children is rarely, if ever, pleasing to our Father. It is certainly not my place, nor my desire to judge or condemn anyone. I do believe, however, that if our churches were comprised of Bible-believing, God-honoring, Spirit-filled Christians, we would see few if any disputes among the brethren.

I feel so strongly about this subject that "Ask Daily for the Infilling of the Holy Spirit" was almost the "A" chapter in the PLAY NICE acronym, but I decided to put it here instead. We see far too much conflict and inappropriate behavior in our churches today. So much of this is because many are striving to do life on their own terms and in their own strength, when they can and should be seeking God's will for them. Doing that seems to me to be about as foolhardy as trying to fly to a distant city by flapping your arms rather than using a plane.

I choose to believe what Jesus said as recorded in John 15:5: "Yes, I am the vine; you are the branches. Those who remain in Me, and I in them, will produce much fruit. For apart from Me, you can do nothing." It seems we see a whole lot of people work very hard doing nothing.

One last note: my friend Pastor Jim Brauer suggested I include something suggesting that many churches have plenty of members but not nearly enough disciples—there is a significant difference between the two. Perhaps you've heard the expression that a statesman cares about the next generation; a politician cares about the next election? Is it too far a stretch to say that a disciple cares about the Body of Christ and about serving His purposes; a church member cares only about their own salvation? A disciple is also one who has yielded to God fully and daily seeks the infilling of the Holy Spirit into all areas of their life. Oh that our churches would have more disciples than mere members, and indeed far less conflict.

CHAPTER CHALLENGE: Take some time this week to be alone with God and do as David did. As we read in Psalm 139:23–24, he prayed, "Search me, O God, and know my heart; test me and know my anxious thoughts. Point out anything in me that offends you, and lead me along the path of everlasting life."

Form the habit of daily, and often throughout the day, inviting God to fill you with His Holy Spirit. Offer yourself to Him in full and complete surrender, and be totally willing for Him to have full control over you.

Section Two:
LOVE YOURSELF AS YOU LOVE YOUR NEIGHBOR

Key text: Romans 13:9: "For the commandments say, 'You must not commit adultery. You must not murder. You must not steal. You must not covet.' These and other such commandments are summed up in this one commandment: 'Love your neighbor as yourself.'"

Quote: *"If God had a refrigerator, your picture would be on it."*

—Max Lucado

My editor asked me the same question you're asking: "Ron, don't you have the title of this chapter backward?" I assured her, as I assure you, that I chose my wording intentionally. In Matthew 22:37–39, we read, "Jesus replied, 'You must love the Lord your God with all your heart, all your soul, and all your mind. This is the first and greatest commandment. A second is equally important: Love your neighbor as yourself.'" Most Christians will agree that this is a requirement from the Lord for living a life of faithfulness to Him.

To be a true follower of Jesus Christ, you must love God *and* love your neighbor. But have you ever considered that this might also be a prophecy? Could it also be true that you will love your neighbor to the extent and in the same way that you love yourself? Might it also be true that you will respect others, admire others, accept others, be patient and tolerant of others, etc. as you do with yourself?

And therein, my friend, lies a major problem for humanity. While I may or may not know you personally, I feel confident to make an assumption about you that all your life you have heard a negative voice in your mind. You have entertained thoughts of comparison with others and often found yourself on the losing side. You have been critical of yourself in ways that if you were to do so with your friends, you would soon find yourself friendless. You have all too often thought you do not measure up, and at times considered that God might love everyone else, but He could not possibly love you since you have messed up so frequently.

By the way, if this resonates with you, please know you are in excellent company. Dr. Robert Firestone and his daughter Dr. Lisa Firestone have researched and popularized a concept they call the CIV—Critical Inner Voice. Again, we all share this less-than-wonderful aspect of humanity. If you knew some of the thoughts that come into my mind each day, you would have nothing to do with me, and you certainly would have no desire to read this book.

There are two reasons for my confidence in making this assumption about you. One is that you and I share a common enemy. He is known by various titles such as satan, the devil, the accuser of the brethren, the dragon, the serpent, and a roaring lion. Think what you may of him, but know this for sure: he hates you and wants nothing more than to destroy you and take you with him to his ultimate destination. He is relentless and far more successful than he ought to be.

You find one of my favorite titles for satan in John 8:44, where Jesus confronted the religious leaders of His day by saying, "For you are the children of your father the devil, and you love to do the evil things he does. He was a murderer from the beginning. He has always hated the truth because there is no truth in him. When he lies, it is consistent with his character; for he is a liar and *the father of lies"* [italics supplied].

If you often hear condemning thoughts in your mind, please recognize the efforts of the enemy to steal your joy and then commit Romans 8:1, 2 to your memory. There you will be assured that "there is no condemnation for those who belong to Christ Jesus." You'll also be reminded that "because you belong to Him, the power of the life-giving Spirit has freed you from the power of sin that leads to death." (Feel free to stop reading and do a little celebratory dance if you are so inclined.)

In the old Pogo comic strip, one of the characters said, "We have met the enemy, and he is us." While I believe there is some truth in that statement, you simply must be aware of the true enemy in your life and not let him influence you to do his bidding. Whenever you hear thoughts in your mind which you know, or have ample reason to suspect are not of God, do as Paul directed in 2 Corinthians 10:5, and take those thoughts captive to the Mind of Christ.

You might also find it helpful to challenge thoughts that come into your mind by asking is this "OG or NOG"–"*Of God*" or "*Not of God?*" The answer to that question should help you determine your next course of action.

The second basis for my assumption that you, like I, entertain negative thoughts in your mind on a regular basis, is that you are what my friend, the late Jack Fowler referred to as an "FHB"–a *Fallible Human Being*. Face it, you have a long history of mishaps, shortcomings, and failures, just as we all do. The problem is that you have too often labeled yourself by your actions rather than accepting them as a normal part of life. You have confused who you are with what you did, or perhaps failed to do. Rather than say, "I failed," you more likely said—or heard—"I'm a failure."

For an excellent secular perspective on accepting your vulnerability and capacity to mess up on occasion, please check out the work of Brené Brown. I so appreciate her quote: "Imperfections are not inadequacies; they are reminders that we're all in this together." Ms. Brown has researched and written wonderful books on the subject of vulnerability. You can also listen to her via her inspiring TED Talks. Rather than try to hide your imperfections, Ms. Brown encourages, embrace and accept them as a part of who you are. By doing so, you take away their ability to put you down and leave you discouraged.

So, what, you may ask, does all this have to do with preventing conflict in the Church? I'm so glad you asked. Once you accept who you are in Christ, you will be much more able to accept others (see Section Three). When you are at peace with yourself, you will find it far easier to live in peace with others. People with Christ in their lives can and should be the most tolerant, accepting, forgiving, loving, joyful, peaceful people on the planet. What's that old song? "They will know we are Christians by our love." I dare say that love should extend to yourself as well as to others. If you are a believer in Christ, you have the assurance of salvation and peace with God, so all else pales in comparison and significance.

In closing, I believe Christians sometimes have a hard time loving themselves for fear they will become proud and self-aggrandizing. That might help explain why Christians, in particular, find it difficult to accept a compliment with a simple thank you. They go out of their way to downplay or diminish their role or participation. Someone once shared with me that whenever you receive praise or a compliment, acknowledge the comment with a simple thank you. Don't make too much of it *or* too little. Consider the comment as a rose, which is yours to enjoy. Throughout the day as you may collect other compliments, simply add them to the bouquet. Just be sure that before you go to sleep at night, you lift the bouquet up to Jesus and thank Him for using you that day and for allowing you to receive such appreciative thoughts. Giving Christ credit for how you were used or what you accomplished is the best way I know of to protect against your ego taking the credit.

Nelson Mandela is often credited (although it may have actually been self-help guru Marianne Williamson) with having said, "Our deepest fear is not that we are inadequate. Our deepest fear is that we are powerful beyond measure. It is our light, not our darkness that most frightens us. We ask ourselves, 'Who am I to be brilliant, gorgeous, talented, fabulous?' Actually, who are you not to be? You are a child of God. Your playing small doesn't serve the world. There's nothing enlightened about shrinking so that other people won't feel insecure around you. It's not just in some of us, it's in everyone, and as we let our light shine, we unconsciously give other people permission to do the same. As we are liberated from our fear, our presence automatically liberates others."

Please reread that quote. Work to believe it applies to you. My hope is that you will find yourself more at peace with God. Once there, you have every right to be at peace with yourself and be much better able to be at peace with, and love, others. Bob George, in *Growing in Grace*, puts it this way: "Our relationship to God carries over directly into our human relationships. We will ultimately treat others in exactly the same way we think God treats us."

Think for a moment of someone you admire. Would you consider them to be, as they say, "comfortable in their own skin?" The answer likely is yes, and as a Christian, you have every right to be comfortable with who you are, especially as you realize Whose you are!

And, if you'll permit me one more Bible citation, Rom 5:1 reads, "Therefore, since we have been made right in God's sight by faith, we have peace with God because of what Jesus Christ our Lord has done for us." Time for another dance, perhaps?

CHAPTER CHALLENGE: Strive to replace the CIV with CPV (Complimentary Positive Voice) You are God's masterpiece (see Ephesians 2:10 NLT).

Please do not take what you have just read too far, however, and fall into the trap of thinking *too* highly of yourself. Trust me. God hates pride, and He has ways of letting you know of His displeasure. We'll look to balance the equation in the chapter on humility, Chapter A2. As with so many other aspects of life, beware of extremes. Strive to find the right balance between humility and self-love and acceptance.

CHAPTER L1:

If You Don't Do This, Who Will?

Key text: 1 Corinthians 6:19, 20: "Don't you realize that your body is the temple of the Holy Spirit, Who lives in you and was given to you by God? You do not belong to yourself, for God bought you with a high price. So you must honor God with your body."

Quote: *"If my body is the temple of Holy Spirit, why do I so often treat it as an amusement park?"*

—Source unknown

realize I am dating myself big time when I tell you I remember a song titled "Button Up Your Overcoat" sung by Ruth Etting. One part of that song that stands out to me is "Take good care of yourself—you belong to me." As you just read in this chapter's key text, those words could easily come to you from God Himself.

With that said, I wonder why it is that we often take such poor care of our bodies when this is our only abode this side of Heaven. We all say we long for Heaven, but some of us seem to be in an awfully big hurry to get there.

As I wrote about in the previous chapter, I believe most of us have a difficult time loving and accepting ourselves as God would have us do, and nowhere is this perhaps best exemplified than in how we take care of ourselves. And how, you may ask, is this relevant in a book on preventing and resolving conflict in the Church? Simply because the better health you enjoy, the better you will be able to manage conflict. If you are too often tired, stressed, poorly nourished, etc., you will not be at your best, and you will far more likely get entangled in situations that you might have otherwise prevented. You will also likely lack the necessary mindset and ability to address conflict in a God-honoring and productive manner.

And just to remove any doubt you may have, let me assure you that you are worth taking care of, for as we read in 1 Peter 1:18–19: "For you know that God paid a ransom to save you from the empty life you inherited from your ancestors. And it was not paid with mere gold or silver, which lose their value. It was the precious blood of Christ, the sinless, spotless Lamb of God."

Americans are said to be among the most obese and out-of-shape people on the planet. And why is this the case? Certainly, it is not due to a lack of information. Books and resources on healthful living abound in our society. It can't be due to an insufficient supply of healthy foods. In that area, we are the envy of the world.

Again, information and guidelines for optimal health are readily available to any who choose to seek them out. I would caution you that not all such resources are equal and, at least in my humble opinion, some are more harmful than beneficial. While I do not intend to go into specifics about health resources, I do want to share with you an easy-to-understand and somewhat easy-to-follow model. It's called CLEANSTART, developed by my friend Ron Johnson.

CLEANSTART is an acronym for ten components you should consider and address if you really want to operate at peak physical, mental, emotional, and spiritual levels.

"C" stands for Clean water;

"L" advocates for Loving relationships;

"E" is for regular Exercise;

"A" equals Air–fresh air, that is;

"N" you might guess is Nutrition;

"S" calls for adequate but measured Sunshine;

"T" reminds us to practice Temperance (or moderation);

"A" represents an Attitude of Gratitude;

"R" signifies Rest; and

"T" though last is certainly not least–Trust in God

As you look over that list, you may regard each component as simply being common sense, but in this case, as in so many others, is common sense always common practice? I believe the answer here is a resounding "Duh, I don't think so!"

Ron combined each of these elements with specific Bible verses to emphasize the point that God wants you to be healthy. In this area, His Word is clear, His desires without debate. The only question that remains then is what part will you play in cooperating with His plan? To get a full copy of Ron Johnson's CLEANSTART model, with Biblical citations, you can request it from him at sweetpilgrim@yahoo.com.

CHAPTER CHALLENGE: Resolve that you will pay more attention to your overall health and wellness. Consider three of the CLEANSTART areas to focus on for the next few weeks, and then look to add others. If you try to do too much at once, you will likely fall short, get discouraged, and resort to old, unhealthy practices. Get a coach if you feel that would be helpful, or perhaps an accountability partner who also wants to be healthier. Don't worry about the results. Just focus on the process, and the results will take care of themselves.

Also, be sure to check out the Bonus/Call to Action page at the end of this book for details on how you can enroll in a free mini-course on Relationship CPR (Conflict Prevention & Resolution)

CHAPTER L2:

Who Are You Anyway?

Key text: John 1: 12, 13: "But to all who believed Him (Christ) and accepted Him, He gave the right to become children of God. They are reborn—not with a physical birth resulting from human passion or plan, but a birth that comes from God."

Quote: *"There are plenty of obstacles in your path. Don't allow yourself to become one of them."*

—Ralph Marston

A parable is told about an eagle who was wounded while young and picked up by a local farmer. The farmer nursed the eagle back to health and let it feed and grow with his chickens. Many days the eagle would look up to the sky and enviously watch an eagle soar by. In between bites of his chicken feed, the eagle would bemoan his condition and silently wish he could be an eagle.

31

A somewhat silly story, I admit, but one with an important question: was he an eagle or a chicken? My answer to that question is that by birthright and position he was an eagle, but by his condition, he was a chicken. Could we Christians face a similar predicament?

When a person accepts Christ as Lord, is he or she a saint or a sinner? Is their old nature genuinely dead as the Bible says, and if so, why does it appear so alive so often? 2 Corinthians 5:14–17 reads, "Either way, Christ's love controls us. Since we believe that Christ died for all, we also believe that we have all died to our old life. He died for everyone so that those who receive his new life will no longer live for themselves. Instead, they will live for Christ, who died and was raised for them. So, we have stopped evaluating others from a human point of view. At one time, we thought of Christ merely from a human point of view. How differently we know him now! This means that anyone who belongs to Christ has become a new person. The old life is gone; a new life has begun!"

Much like the eagle/chicken, I believe many Christians have an identity crisis. Part of the problem is that when we first accept Christ, we set about to try to live for Him. That sounds good, but is it? If you are trying to live for Him, whose efforts are you relying upon? When you fail, which we all know you frequently will, who gets the blame? When you succeed, who gets the credit?

It might be helpful to study Gal 2:20, where the Apostle Paul wrote, "My old self has been crucified with Christ. It is no longer I who live, but Christ lives in me. So I live in this earthly body by trusting in the Son of God, who loved me and gave himself for me." Christ died that you might be forgiven for your sins—amen? But is that the only reason that He died?

I believe His purpose was also that you might invite Him to live in and through you to serve His purposes. But somehow, you, like so many of us, may have come to believe that you must make yourself acceptable to God, that you must root out sin from your life before that can happen.

If so, your focus will be on your behavior and performance to see how you measure up and that, my friend, could explain why so many Christians miss the joy and peace that Christ promised to all who would accept Him as Lord.

Writing to Timothy (and us) about people in the last days of earth's history, Paul talks of people who will "act religious, but they will reject the power that could make them godly" (2 Timothy 3:5). Our position in Christ is that of overcomer and slave to righteousness. Our condition, all too often, is that of failure and slave to sin. That sure sounds like an identity crisis to me.

Another common problem we share is that we confuse failing with being a failure. Failing only points out the reality that you were born with a birth defect—sin. Over the years you, like the rest of us, have developed attitudes, habits, and practices accordingly. These aspects of your life were not instantly removed when you died to Christ, but the good news is they lost their power over you. It is not your job to overcome your tendencies to sin; in fact, you are powerless to do so. You may, however, let Christ, through the indwelling Holy Spirit, do His work of transformation in you to accomplish that result.

In His Sermon on the Mount, as recorded in Matthew 5:48, Jesus tells His followers that "you are to be perfect, even as your Father in Heaven is perfect." Before you get hung up on that seemingly impossible goal, please know that many Bible commentators consider the word "perfect" to mean "mature." You might also want to remember Matthew 19:26 where Jesus said, "humanly speaking, it is impossible. But with God, everything is possible." One condition you must have in place for this to apply to your life is that you believe that everything Jesus and the Bible said about you is true. You must accept that while you have a history of sin and misdeeds, you are indeed a "new creature in Christ."

I'm reminded of a story I heard many years ago about a mayor's son who spent a night in riotous, illegal activities. The next day, a rival member of the city council came to the mayor, almost gleeful that his son had caused him so much embarrassment. The councilman really poured it on about how disgraceful the son's behavior was. He concluded by declaring, "if he were my son, I'd get rid of him," to which the mayor replied, "I would too—if he was your son." Citing a promise first made in Deuteronomy 31:6, the writer of Hebrews reminds us that "God has said, 'I will never fail you. I will never abandon you'" (Hebrews 13:5).

One reason this is so important to conflict prevention is that when you find yourself on the receiving end of apparent offenses, you do not need to take them so personally. You need no longer be concerned about what others think of you. In fact, what others think of you is really none of your business unless you're going out of your way to create in them a negative impression of you. Christ's opinion of you is what matters—not others' opinion, not even your own.

Entrepreneur and author Dean Graziano tells a story of a missionary who returned from the mission field elated over where he had been and what he had experienced, but he soon became lethargic and apathetic about life. He did not enjoy any of the former experiences that brought him joy and happiness. He was urged to see a doctor, and he learned he had picked up a parasite while in the mission field. Medication was prescribed, and in due time, he was cured and back to his old self. Please don't let parasites of limiting beliefs, attacks from fellow church members, or from the enemy into your life to steal your joy, peace, and contentment—all of which are part of your birthright as a child of God.

You have a choice to make. You are either going to believe what the Bible says about you is true or you are not. You will either rely on its teachings or on the deceptions of the *great liar*. Commercial pilots are trained to fly by instruments, not their feelings. It seems wise to me that we should all determine that we will live by the Truth as found in the Word of God.

CHAPTER CHALLENGE: Do an online search using terms such as "New Life in Christ Bible verses" or something similar. This week, memorize two or three of these attributes of your identity in Christ, and claim them as your own. Next week, select two or three more, and continue this pattern for the next several weeks.

CHAPTER L3:

A Right Way and Lots of Wrong Ways?

Key text: 2 Corinthians 1:3–5: "All praise to God, the Father of our Lord Jesus Christ. God is our merciful Father and the source of all comfort. He comforts us in all our troubles so that we can comfort others. When they are troubled, we will be able to give them the same comfort God has given us. For the more we suffer for Christ, the more God will shower us with his comfort through Christ."

Quote: *"Try to be a rainbow to somebody's cloud."*

—Maya Angelou

A friend of mine recently shared a story of a time when his wife suffered a traumatic loss, and her church family was no help at all. She was 16 at the time when her brother took his life. Can you put yourself in her situation? Can you begin to imagine the grief, confusion, and despair she must have felt? Might this have been a time for the

Body of Christ to rally around her and help her get through this agonizing time? The obvious answer to that last question is yes. The unfortunate reality is that the church did nothing. They basically shunned her, which served to compound her grief. It shouldn't surprise you that now, though decades later, she still harbors bitterness and resentment, and she has never set foot in that church again.

I heard another story of a couple who got divorced, and the husband told his church family to have nothing to do with his now-ex-wife. Did the church family refuse his request and reach out to minister to both parties? You can probably guess the answer is no. They rejected the woman, even going so far as to ignore her and turn away when they saw her in public. They treated her as an outcast, which she was—not by her doing, but by theirs.

You have likely heard horror stories of well-meaning but utterly insensitive Christians who have gone to a grieving mother and tried to comfort her by saying, "Well God must have needed your baby more than you did." Tales abound of times when church members approached a victim of a fire or some other disaster and asked, "Is there unconfessed sin in your life that might have caused God to do this to you?" I do not condone violence, but if I were on the receiving end of such "helpful" remarks, the thought of justifiable homicide would likely cross my mind. Certainly a defense of temporary insanity would stand up in court, don't you think?

Again, though these comments are typically made with the best of intentions, they rarely accomplish their purpose. When their friends or loved ones experience grief, most people feel the need to say something, so the fact that they have no clue what to say does not prevent them from saying it anyway. Most often, unless you are especially close to the person who is grieving, please don't feel you *have* to say anything. Usually, when you don't know what to say, the best course is to say nothing. If you don't believe me, read Proverbs 17:27–28, where Solomon wrote, "A truly wise person uses few words; a person with understanding is even-tempered. Even fools are thought wise when they keep silent; with their mouths shut, they seem intelligent."

I heard a story about a family that suffered a huge loss. Their teenage child was in a horrific accident and was rushed to the hospital. Their pastor was informed of the situation, and he hurried to be with the family. The pastor was especially close to this family, and when they received the news that the child died, he broke down and cried with them. Later that day, the pastor berated himself for his inability to provide comfort and support to the family and that he was unable to somehow lessen their grief. He entertained thoughts of leaving the ministry for which he was obviously so unqualified.

Some months later, the family moved to another state. A few years after that, they came back for a visit and told the pastor how much they appreciated him being with them on the day their child died. The pastor was taken aback by their comment as he vividly remembered how he had "failed" them in their time of need. He told them he regretted not being able to give them any words of hope, comfort, or encouragement. They quickly replied that at that moment, they did not need nor would they have received any of that. They told the pastor that when he cried with them, they knew beyond doubt that he cared deeply for them, and that, they said, was what they needed most.

Grief and loss are a natural part of life on this sin-filled planet. They were not part of God's original plan for us, but He now uses them for our character development. Several verses in Scripture remind us that in our moments of darkness and despair, we can grow into a maturity that we might not otherwise attain (see James 1: 2–3; Romans 5:3–5). So often when we see a brother or sister who is hurting, we want to alleviate their pain, but when someone you care about is carrying a burden, please do not feel the need to remove that burden. You may be stepping in the way of what God wants to do for them in that situation.

So what should you do when a brother or sister is grieving? First off, consider your motive and intent. If you are looking to assuage your own pain and grief, please stay home. I can just about promise you that you will do more harm than good. You are not the Holy Spirit, and no one expects you to be.

Prayer is always appropriate, especially when you intercede on behalf of the person that they will be ministered to by "the God of all comfort." (2 Cor 1:3). In situations like this, you likely lack wisdom for what to say or do. James 1:5 reads, "If you need wisdom, ask our generous God, and He will give it to you." That sure sounds like wise counsel to me.

One last thought. Please know that there are times in everyone's life when he or she is not at their best. Times of grief and hardship certainly fall in that category. These situations can cause people to be super sensitive and reactionary. Hopefully, this awareness will help you or them to refrain from taking offense when someone tries but fails to add comfort and consolation.

CHAPTER CHALLENGE: When someone you know experiences loss or hardship, pause before you decide what you should or should not say or do. In the words of the ancient Greek physician Hippocrates: "First, do no harm." Consider sending a card or conveying to them in some way that you do care and that you are lifting them up in prayer. Call a family member to see if they would appreciate help with a meal, childcare, or some other felt need.

Section Three:
ACCEPT OTHERS

Key text: Colossians 3:12–15: "Since God chose you to be the holy people he loves, you must clothe yourselves with tenderhearted mercy, kindness, humility, gentleness, and patience. Make allowance for each other's faults, and forgive anyone who offends you. Remember, the Lord forgave you, so you must forgive others. Above all, clothe yourselves with love, which binds us all together in perfect harmony. And let the peace that comes from Christ rule in your hearts. For as members of one body, you are called to live in peace. And always be thankful."

Quote: *"To live above with the ones we love, o that will be glory! But to live below with the ones we know, now that's a different story."*

—Author unknown

I don't know about other cultures, but it sure seems to me that we Americans are obsessed with self-help books, courses, retreats, etc. Go into almost any bookstore, and chances are the most extensive section you'll see will be devoted to books which promise to tell you how you can have more of what you think you want from life and less of what you find objectional. I appreciate the Frank and Ernest comic strip I read several years back: one of them walked into a bookstore and asked for the book *How to Stop Buying Self-Help Books, Volume Seven.*

Please don't get me wrong. I'm not at all opposed to people striving to improve their lives. It seems to be an obsession for some, but who am I to judge? I also believe that all personal striving is doomed to fail if not directed and empowered by the Holy Spirit, but that's a subject for another chapter.

In the 1960s, Thomas Anthony Harris wrote *I'm Okay, You're Okay.* Initially published in 1967, it became a widespread success in the '70s, staying on the *New York Times* bestseller list for two years. Today, unfortunately, a far-too-common sentiment in some churches seems to be "I'm Okay, You're Not!" or "You're Okay, I'm Not!" As I mentioned in the Love Yourself chapter, there may be a reasonable explanation for either of these philosophies, but based on the Word of God there certainly cannot be an excuse for them.

Even a cursory reading of the Bible will convince you that God wants His children to get along with each other, to accept each other, and to work together for the common good of all. Being in conflict or holding each other in contempt is not endorsed in any Bible book or chapter I've yet found. Though I haven't counted myself, I have reason to believe there are over 50 "one another" verses in the King James Version of the Bible, which tell us how we are to treat each other. Some of these verses include *Love* one another (John 13:34); *Pray for* one another (Ephesians 6:18); *Serve* one another (Galatians 5:13); *Confess* your sins *to* one another (James 5:16); etc.

In 1 Corinthians 12, the Apostle Paul paints a vivid picture of how churches are to function to fulfill God's purpose for them. He details how the Holy Spirit gives different gifts to each member, and he emphasizes that all gifts are necessary to make a complete Church. Surely some gifts may receive more notoriety and acclaim than others, but each should be regarded as essential to the overall health and welfare of the Church, which Scripture often refers to as the Body of Christ.

To be sure we get the picture, Paul goes on to compare the Church body to the human body. I can almost see him chuckling to himself as he poses absurd questions such as: "If the whole body were an eye, how would you hear? Or if your whole body were an ear, how would you smell anything?" (1 Corinthians 12:17). I love the illustration I first heard from resiliency expert and professional speaker Eileen McDargh. She drew a picture of a rowboat with two people in it. The boat was tilting as a hole had developed near the front. While the person in the front was bailing like crazy, the person in the back folded his arms and proclaimed, "I'm glad that hole isn't on *my* side of the boat." Perhaps you've heard the expression, "We're all in the same boat." And of all institutions, should not this be true of God's Church?

But alas and alack (wow when is the last time you heard that expression?) churches are composed of human beings who have not yet been made perfect. I believe we all have some degree of Post Traumatic Stress Disorder. Truly some have more severe cases than others, but most all of us have memories of times we were treated in ways we should not have been or times when we were not treated in ways we should have been. Some of these experiences caused a degree of trauma. Since we are past those experiences now and since we still remember them vividly, we could rightly say we have Post Traumatic Stress. Most of us function well despite this commonly shared ailment, while others require help to keep it from becoming a disorder and ruling their lives.

Along with sharing this condition, we each also have a sinful nature that far too often thinks he or she is still in control of our lives. For the spiritual Christian, this sinful nature has been replaced with a new nature, and as we read in Romans 6:6, the old nature is dead. I know that's what Scripture says, but doesn't it seem at times that the old nature never got the memo that it has been replaced? This being the case, should it surprise you that at times church members might turn on each other and become embroiled in conflict, or treat each other in less-than-favorable ways? Paul chastises the Corinthian church for such behavior in 1 Corinthians 3. We would be well served to heed his counsel today.

Gary Thomas wrote *Sacred Marriage*—a book I highly recommend. I am intrigued by the subtitle: "What if God designed marriage to make us holy more than to make us happy?" Wow, what a concept! And would it be too much of a stretch to pose the same question about the Church? What if God designed the Church to be a living laboratory where we could practice Christlike love and selflessness? What if our church experience equipped us not just to tolerate differences in others but to value and appreciate them?

Secular psychologist and creator of Client-Centered Therapy, Carl Rogers, wrote: "I have found it of enormous value when I can permit myself to understand the other person. The way in which I have worded this statement may seem strange to you. Is it necessary to permit oneself to understand another?" He goes on to say, "I think it is. Our first reaction to most of the statements which we hear from other people is an evaluation or a judgment rather than an understanding of it. When someone expresses some feeling, attitude or belief, our tendency is almost immediately to feel 'that's right' or 'that's stupid,' 'that's abnormal,' 'that's unreasonable,' 'that's correct,' or that is—or is not—very nice.'" He concludes his thought by saying, "Very rarely do we permit ourselves to understand precisely what the meaning of the statement is *to the other person*" [emphasis added].

To further illustrate the need to understand and accept each other, here's a thought I got from a marriage enrichment source but cannot remember where: "Behind every behavior is a present intention. I see only my intention, not my behavior. You only see my behavior, not my intention. Therefore, you react to my behavior, not my intention. I need to clarify my intentions to you, and you need to give me feedback on how my behavior impacts you, and we both have to believe each other."

That sounds a lot like 1 Samuel 16:7 to me: "The Lord doesn't see things the way you see them. People judge by outward appearance, but the Lord looks at the heart." Can you see how that could dramatically improve a couple's ability to have a successful marriage? What if church members were to do the same with each other? Can you see how so many conflicts could be prevented before they ever had a chance to develop?

Nobody, God included, ever said life would be easy or that humans would always walk in harmony with each other. But easy or not, that is exactly what I believe God wants for us, His children. He deserves it, and so do we. You might find it helpful to remember the words spoken by the late Pastor Adrian Rogers: "Yes I'm a nut, but I'm fastened to a perfect Bolt." Amen?

CHAPTER CHALLENGE: Make it a specific part of your daily prayer life to ask God to help you be more loving and accepting of others. Consider church members whom you could reach out to in some way to let them know you appreciate them and that you are glad they are part of the church family.

Listen to the Babbie Mason song "What in the World Did He Save Us For?" and apply the message to your life. Another good song to hear would be Karen Peck's song "Why Can't All God's Children Get Along?"

EXTRA CREDIT BIBLE TEXTS:

James 5:9

1 John 4:7–8

1 Thessalonians 5:15

1 Peter 4:7–8

Ephesians 4:31–32

1 Corinthians 13:3
James 4:11, 12
Ephesians 4:1–7

Is This Always Your Best Choice?

Key text: Proverbs 17:9: "Love prospers when a fault is forgiven, but dwelling on it separates close friends."

Quote: *"As long as you don't forgive, who and whatever it is will occupy a rent-free space in your mind."*

—Isabell Holland

A s I have written a time or two, okay maybe three, conflict between humans who regularly associate together is inevitable. That may be a bit of a stretch, but it is certainly true for the vast majority of us. If you have people in your life who are important to you, people you care about, sooner or later they are going to offend, disappoint, or frustrate you in some way. You then have a decision to make. A decision, I might add, with serious consequences attached.

You may choose to hold their offense against them and seek to exact revenge or payback. You may choose to dwell on the offense and harbor resentment toward them. Ultimately, you may decide to sever your connection with them. Were you to choose this course, you certainly would not be the first to do so, and in my humble opinion, it is the most appropriate choice in certain situations. I am also of the opinion that this option is chosen far too quickly and far too often in our society.

Since you are reading a book about conflict in the Church, I will assume you have at least some interest in living your life based on the Word of God, and in following your Savior Jesus Christ. If that is the case, your only option is to forgive the person who wronged you. You may determine that the relationship is too damaged to be continued, which again may be the kindest path to take for both of you. While I absolutely believe Christians are to forgive others who offend us, I do not believe we are necessarily called to put ourselves in situations where we know we will be mistreated on a recurring basis.

Much more could be said on that subject, and of course, circumstances will determine the proper course of action in any given situation. For now, let's focus on the constant that we find in wellness literature— both Biblical and secular—that forgiveness is the only path to happiness, contentment, and the avoidance of conflict. You may be familiar with the numerous Bible texts which clearly detail the duty of every Christian to extend forgiveness to those who offend them. But did you know that such esteemed institutions as Johns Hopkins Medicine and the Mayo Clinic have posted information on the health benefits of forgiveness? If you do a search for health benefits of forgiveness, you will find numerous articles for further study.

By doing this research, you will come to the conclusion that granting forgiveness is not just a nice thing to do, but it is clearly the smartest decision you can make. According to Marianne Williamson, "Unforgiveness is like drinking poison yourself and waiting for the other person to die." I like how the ancient Greek playwright Euripides put it when he said, "Waste not fresh tears over old griefs." In more modern times, life coach and motivational speaker Mary Manin Morrissey believes "The energy it takes to hang on to the past is holding you back from a new life." Or, lastly, how about the Irish proverb which reads, "Even a small thorn causes festering."

There are so many more quotes I could cite that extol the benefits and wisdom of choosing to forgive others, but space limitations prohibit me from listing them all. For now, I want to highlight a few aspects of forgiveness that I believe will serve you well in preventing potential conflicts with church members.

First, you must understand that forgiveness does not mean you forget what the other person did to you. The old expression "forgive and forget" may sound sweet and wise, but short of brain injury, it is not humanly possible. In case you don't believe me, pause for a moment and recall the name of your first- or second-grade teacher. For some of you, that exercise took you back several years, but my hunch is that their names or faces came readily to the forefront of your mind. The point I make is that you cannot force yourself to forget something that has been imbedded in your mind. If you challenge yourself to connect forgiveness with forgetfulness, you are bound to experience failure and frustration.

Granting forgiveness to someone is a decision you make to not hold against them what they did to you. You decide to let it go, and rather than forgive and forget, you choose to forgive and move on. Oprah Winfrey says, "True forgiveness is when you can say 'thank you for that experience.'" That may be a bit of a stretch for some, but I like the sentiment.

On a humorous note, I have long appreciated a story I heard about a lady who had been grievously wronged by a fellow church member. After a time, she decided to forgive the offender, and she told a friend of her decision. Aghast, the friend asked, "How can you forgive her—don't you remember what she did to you?"

The lady replied, "No, I specifically remember forgetting that."

And for one last bit of humor . . . American writer Ivern Ball wrote, "Most of us can forgive and forget; we just don't want the other person to forget that we forgave."

All humor aside, forgiveness is no laughing matter. The Bible is absolutely clear that it is not optional for the believer. Numerous passages indicate, without a doubt, that you will be forgiven only to the extent that you willingly forgive others. But required or not, granting forgiveness is difficult in some circumstances when you feel great pain or displeasure over what someone has done to you. So, along with separating forgiveness from forgetfulness, you must also separate how you feel from deciding to do what you know is right. As Zig Ziglar used to teach, logic will not change an emotion, but action will. When you have been wronged or offended in some way, you simply must choose to forgive regardless of how you feel, and regardless of whether the offending party asks for your forgiveness or not. Wait, what did you just read?

In a perfect church, anyone who offends you will realize their wrong and quickly and sincerely come to you confessing their fault, and they will ask for your forgiveness. As I said, that would always be the case in a perfect church. Of course, I guess in a perfect church, there would be no offending in the first place. But, since churches are composed of imperfect people, you cannot expect perfect behavior from your fellow church members. You are not responsible for what the offending party does or does not do. You can only, by God's grace and help, determine that you will forgive him or her, and really, what better choice do you have? Writer William Arthur Ward was spot on: "We are most like beasts when we kill. We are most like men when we judge. We are most like God when we forgive."

One reason some might find it difficult to forgive someone is that they have a hard time forgiving themselves. As I wrote in a previous chapter, you will love your neighbor as you love yourself. Might not the same be said that you will forgive your neighbor as you forgive yourself? As humans, we are so hard on ourselves at times. I propose we are too hard on ourselves and in a way that dishonors the God who made us. We are His children, and He is not pleased when we spend time beating ourselves up, literally or figuratively. I urge you to consider the words of American poet Stephen Levine, who said, "Letting ourselves be forgiven is one of the most difficult healings we will undertake. And one of the most fruitful."

Please also remember the words of the 19th century British preacher Charles Spurgeon: "God is more willing to forgive than you are to sin." I'm confident in saying those words apply to you as well as to any who might do you wrong—ya think?

CHAPTER CHALLENGE: Ken Sande, the former director of Peacemaker Ministries, wrote *The Peacemaker: A Biblical Guide to Resolving Personal Conflict.* In the book, he details the Seven As of Confession and the Four Promises of Forgiveness. You might want to download a copy of each by searching for Ken Sande Relational Wisdom 360.

EXTRA CREDIT BIBLE TEXTS:

Psalms 65:3; 86:5; 103:3

Mt. 6:9–15; 18:21–35

Lk. 17:4

Rom. 4:4–8

Ephesians 4:31–32

Col. 3:12–15

1 Peter 2:21–23

1 John 1:9

Want More of God's Grace? Here's how you get it.

Key text: Phillipians 2:3: "Don't be selfish; don't try to impress others. Be humble, thinking of others as better than yourself."

Quote*: "A humble person is not one who thinks little of himself, hangs his head and says, 'I'm nothing.' Rather, he is one who depends wholly on the Lord for everything, in every circumstance."*

—David Wilkerson

My wife and I thoroughly enjoyed our honeymoon in Orlando, Florida, in December 1980. Of course, you can't visit Orlando without visiting Mickey and his friends at Disney World. At that time, the Magic Kingdom was the only theme park in operation, and we spent two days there. Trust me when I tell you we got our money's worth. We got there reasonably early each day and were among the last to exit the park at night.

There were two ways to get from the park to the parking lot. You could either ride the ferry boat or the monorail. Since it was late December, we opted for the warmth and comfort of the monorail. Unfortunately, when we got to the monorail station, the line in front of us was huge—at least for the section marked "Parking Lot." There was another line that was basically empty. It read, "Expensive hotels that you cannot afford." Okay, it didn't really say that, but it might as well have. If you were staying on property, you got the fringe benefit of getting quicker access to the monorail.

I remembered that after leaving the park, the monorail stopped at the Cosmopolitan Hotel and then continued on to the parking lot. I told my new bride to follow me as I had a great idea. Naively and lovingly, she complied, and sure enough, we went right to the front of the line. The monorail arrived in short order and took us to the Cosmopolitan, but we stayed seated and exited at the next stop—the parking lot.

I have to tell you I did not walk to my car that night. I floated. I had just clearly demonstrated to my wife beyond any shadow of a doubt that she had married a genius, a man with enormous brilliance that she was fortunate and blessed enough to partner with for the rest of her life.

The next night, the scenario played out the same way. The line for the parking lot was gigantic, the line for the hotels minuscule. Oh, how I wished I could share my wisdom and enlighten the poor souls in the peasant—I mean parking lot—line, but alas, I could not. With my bride on my arm, we entered the hotel line and again quickly found ourselves riding to the parking lot. When the car stopped at the Cosmopolitan, something was different. The door to our car did not open. Not to worry. We didn't want to get off there anyway. But when the door didn't open at the parking lot either, we had a problem.

What I later discovered was that the car we had inadvertently gotten on that second night was programmed to open at the Polynesian Hotel, which is located just past the stop for the parking lot. We didn't realize that the car opening at the parking lot the previous night had been a fluke. Without realizing there was a difference the previous night, we had again, inadvertently, gotten on a car headed for the Cosmopolitan. Long, long story short, we had to ride all the way back to the beginning, exit the car, and proceed over to the line marked "parking lot." The only good point of this story is that by that time, the line there was pretty much empty.

It says in Proverbs 16:18 that "Pride goes before destruction, and haughtiness before a fall." I learned that night that pride and haughtiness also go before a long monorail ride. By the way, one of my favorite quotes, although I cannot cite the author, is "Those who cannot laugh at themselves leave the job to others."

Under inspiration, the Apostle Peter wrote, "In the same way, you who are younger must accept the authority of the elders. And all of you dress yourselves in humility as you relate to one another, for 'God opposes the proud but gives grace to the humble.' So humble yourselves under the mighty power of God, and at the right time, he will lift you up in honor. Give all your worries and cares to God, for he cares about you. Stay alert! Watch out for your great enemy, the devil. He prowls around like a roaring lion, looking for someone to devour. Stand firm against him, and be strong in your faith. Remember that your family of believers all over the world is going through the same kind of suffering you are" (1 Peter 5:5–9).

We also read in Proverbs 13:10, "Pride leads to conflict; those who take advice are wise." With even a casual reading of Scripture, you can be assured that God hates your pride and delights in your humility. True humility is the right understanding of who you are and Whose you are. It serves as an antidote against self-centeredness, which Larry Crabb calls the root of all sin.

Humility also helps to counter judgmentalism. In a portion of His Sermon on the Mount found in Mathew 7:1–3, Jesus admonishes His followers, "Do not judge others, and you will not be judged. For you will be treated as you treat others. The standard you use in judging is the standard by which you will be judged." He then poses a challenging question: "And why worry about a speck in your friend's eye when you have a log in your own? How can you think of saying to your friend, 'Let me help you get rid of that speck in your eye,' when you can't see past the log in your own eye?" He continues, in no uncertain terms, "Hypocrite! (His word, not mine) First get rid of the log in your own eye; then you will see well enough to deal with the speck in your friend's eye."

Can you imagine what life would be like if more people lived out Christlike humility? I believe each of us would have a closer relationship with God and others. Our churches would likely see little if any conflict. Our communities would see a drastic reduction if not the elimination of divorce and crime, and our world would experience far fewer if any wars. Okay, that might seem utopian, but it is a nice dream, don't you think?

Mohandas Karamchand Gandhi, better known to us as Mahatma Gandhi, is quoted as having said, "There is nothing wrong with Christianity, but how often do we see it in operation?" Ouch, that hurts! Dear reader, there is nothing wrong with genuine humility, but again, how often do we see it in operation? And, perhaps, we do not see more humility because we don't seek it. In Isaiah 66: 2, we read, "My hands have made both heaven and earth; they and everything in them are mine. I, the Lord, have spoken!" He goes on to promise, "I will bless those who have humble and contrite hearts, who tremble at my word."

James exhorts us: "So humble yourselves before God. Resist the devil, and he will flee from you. Come close to God, and God will come close to you. Wash your hands, you sinners; purify your hearts, for your loyalty is divided between God and the world. Let there be tears for what you have done. Let there be sorrow and deep grief. Let there be sadness instead of laughter, and gloom instead of joy. Humble yourselves before the Lord, and he will lift you up in honor" (James 4:7–10).

Do you want God's blessing? Do you desire for God to come close to you? Ideally, those are rhetorical questions, but if your answer is yes, you have no option but to seek and practice humility. Does that mean others might take advantage of you at times? I'd say that is quite likely. Does that mean you won't always get your way? You can count on that one. Will your practice of genuine humility cause you to face unjust treatment at times? For sure! But please take comfort that you are following God's will for you as you'll find in 1 Corinthians 6:7–8: "Even to have such lawsuits with one another is a defeat for you. *Why not just accept the injustice and leave it at that? Why not let yourselves be cheated?* Instead, you yourselves are the ones who do wrong and cheat even your fellow believers" [emphasis added].

I heard a story so long ago that I cannot remember who said what I am about to share, and I may have some of the details wrong. But as my close friends know, I never let facts get in the way of a good story ☺. A man traveling along a road was mugged and relieved of all his valuables. After the incident, he prayed to God and thanked Him that he was not physically hurt by the robber; that all he lost were material items, and lastly he thanked God that it was he who was robbed and not he who was the robber.

That's the kind of humility that I desire—how about you? I long to live a life devoid of self-serving pride and be totally sold out to Jesus Christ, my risen Lord, Savior, and soon-returning King. To do otherwise is to lose out on all He wants me to experience in this life. Pastor A.W. Tozer put it this way: "For the Christian, humility is absolutely indispensable. Without it, there can be no self-knowledge, no repentance, no faith, and no salvation." The Apostle Paul wrote to his disciple Titus,

"They (believers) must not slander anyone and must avoid quarreling. Instead, they should be gentle and show true humility to everyone."

CHAPTER CHALLENGE: Form the habit of regularly asking God to transform you from the inside out, to enable you to live your life from a position of humility. According to Maya Angelou, "If you find it in your heart to care for somebody else, you will have succeeded." I dare say you will also form a great defense against pride and self-centeredness. You will also find yourself preventing much needless conflict with your brothers and sisters.

CHAPTER A3:

How to Destroy a Church

Key text: Psalm 15: 1–3: "A Psalm of David. Who may worship in your sanctuary, LORD? Who may enter your presence on your holy hill? Those who lead blameless lives and do what is right, speaking the truth from sincere hearts. Those who refuse to gossip or harm their neighbors or speak evil of their friends."

Quote: *"Beware of half-truth—you may have gotten hold of the wrong half."*
—Author unknown

A ren't you thankful for the Bible, God's Holy Word, His owner's manual for how we are supposed to do life? It's not just a "do this" or "don't do that" Book, but instead, it provides wisdom and direction for how to be happy and successful in life.

Now, undoubtedly, the Bible does contain warnings against certain behaviors, certain sins. For example, in Romans 1 the Apostle Paul lists many evils that have been committed by man. In verses 28–32, we read, "Since they thought it foolish to acknowledge God, he abandoned them to their foolish thinking and let them do things that should never be done. Their lives became full of every kind of wickedness, sin, greed, hate, envy, murder, quarreling, deception, malicious behavior, and gossip. They are backstabbers, haters of God, insolent, proud, and boastful. They invent new ways of sinning, and they disobey their parents. They refuse to understand, break their promises, are heartless, and have no mercy. They know God's justice requires that those who do these things deserve to die, yet they do them anyway. Worse yet, they encourage others to do them, too."

Wow, there's some vile and totally ungodly behavior on that list—murder, wickedness, haters of God! But did you notice gossip and backstabbing are right smack in the middle of them all? I am firm in my conviction that God hates gossip and backstabbing. He hates it when His children treat each other poorly. He simply will not put up with it, and therefore, neither should we.

Again, it seems so plain to me from this text and many others I could cite that our Father wants us to refrain from gossip, from meddling in others' business, from spreading rumors, and from slandering or speaking poorly of each other. Well then, if this is true, why is it so prevalent in our churches today? While there are several possible reasons, here are a few that I came up with:

Sin still lives in us even though we are born again. In Romans chapter seven, Paul writes about how he occasionally did what he did not want to do and did not do what he did want to do.

Perhaps we feel it somehow makes us look better when we tell others how bad someone else is. We can take comfort that while we're not perfect, at least we're not as bad as so-and-so.

Another explanation could be because we are hurting. As I wrote in *PLAY NICE in Your Sandbox at Work*, hurting people will hurt people.

They don't have to plan it or devise elaborate schemes. If we are hurting, we will take it out on others in some form or fashion. Spreading gossip, rumors, or innuendos certainly fills that bill.

Whatever the reason, I hope you will agree that gossip, rumors, slander, and meddling are just plain wrong, and they should have no place within a church. As followers of the Lord Jesus Christ and members of His Body, we each must do what we can to stop all such behaviors in their proverbial tracks.

And, lest you think these behaviors are somehow a new phenomenon in human interactions, way back in the book of Leviticus God told His people, "Do not spread slanderous gossip among your people." (Leviticus 19:16) In Exodus 23:1 God tells His people, "You must not pass along false rumors. You must not cooperate with evil people by lying on the witness stand."

While you may be surprised to find a chapter on gossip in a book devoted to the prevention and resolution of conflict, I have reason to believe it has been the source of numerous ugly situations in churches that could have easily been prevented. Life is hard at times, and we humans tend to take our frustrations out on others, which can't possibly be pleasing to God or helpful in any way.

Another element of gossip that makes it so distasteful is that you have no idea what's going on in another's life. Some years ago, I watched a video with David Ring, an evangelist who was born with Cerebral Palsy. While his speech is not elegant, his message and impact are outstanding. He preached one message titled "The Suit; things are not always what they seem." At one point in his message, he drew attention to how sharply dressed he was that day. And then he slowly unbuttoned his suit coat and slid it off, revealing a tattered, blood-stained shirt that seemed to have more holes than fabric. After the laughter subsided, he made the compelling point that none of us knows what is going on inside of another person.

You must realize that every one of us faces difficulties and trials of various types, and at various times. How dare we spread rumors or gossip about someone without knowing what's going on inside them? Could this in part explain why God tells us in Matthew 7:1 that we are not to judge lest we ourselves be judged?

Certainly, there are some behaviors that are so unChristlike and so hurtful to the Church that they must be addressed. Galatians 6:1 tells us clearly that we are to go to a brother or sister who is caught up in sin but always with the proper attitude of love and redemption, never condemnation. We are also counseled to be careful that we do not fall into the same trap as they did.

There is also a vast difference between judging someone's behavior and judging them as a person. All too often, I fear, we judge the person more than the behavior. God warns us against doing this as we are so likely to get it wrong. Read 1 Samuel 16:7, where He tells us that we typically don't see things as He sees them. We judge by outer appearance, while only He can know the inner heart.

So maybe this chapter has struck a nerve with you? If so, let me suggest you earnestly seek God's forgiveness and His transforming help that you never engage in such behavior again. It is also likely you need to go to the person(s) you offended, confess your sin, and ask for their forgiveness as well. We all need to regularly seek and receive God's grace and mercy and be ever ready to share those gifts with others.

Your church should be a hospital of sorts where people who are sick and hurting can come to find some relief from their sickness and despair. It should never be a place that adds to people's pain through gossip, judgment, or condemnation.

CHAPTER CHALLENGE: Ask God to reveal to you anyone whom you may have offended through gossip or other unacceptable behavior. Schedule a time to meet with them and offer your apology and request for forgiveness.

Watch Pastor Ring's message in two parts on YouTube.

EXTRA CREDIT BIBLE TEXTS:

Psalm 41:6; 69:12

Proverbs 11:13; 16:28; 17:4, 25:10

2 Corinthians 12:20

1 Timothy 5:13

Section Four:
YIELD TO GOD'S WILL

Key text: Galatians 2:20: "For I have been crucified with Christ, therefore I no longer live. And the life I now live I live by faith in the Son of God Who loved me and gave Himself for me."

Quote: *"The reason some of us are such poor specimens of Christianity is because we have no Almighty Christ. We have Christian attributes and experiences, but there is no abandonment to Jesus Christ."*

—Oswald Chambers

It was October 14, 1979. I was driving from my home in Cortez, Colorado, over the beautiful Rocky Mountains to Denver. The day is etched in my memory as I had been baptized the night before, and I was on a glorious spiritual high not solely due to the elevation. A member of my new church family gave me a cassette tape (you younger readers may have to ask your parents to explain) by a group that I believe was called Harvest. As I neared the top of Wolf Creek Pass (elevation 10,856 ft.), I heard a lyric that took me by surprise.

The chorus to the song was, in part, "for if You're not Lord of everything, then You're not Lord at all." I remember I stopped the tape, and since I only had fast-forward on my player, I ejected the cassette, turned it over, and reinserted. I then hit the fast-forward button for a few seconds, ejected the tape again, and reinserted it to make sure I had heard the words correctly. Guess what? I heard the exact same words the second time: "for if You're not Lord of everything, then You're not Lord at all."

I still remember the conversation the Lord and I had after I stopped the tape. "Really," I asked somewhat incredulously, "if You're not Lord of **everything,** then You're not Lord **at all?**" The conversation lasted several miles before I came to the realization and acceptance of what the chorus meant. If I refused to give each and every aspect of my life to Jesus, then I did not truly regard Him as **Lord** of my life. He might be a really close friend, a very trusted advisor, a wonderful person to hang out with, but He would not be my **Lord**.

If you look up the word *lord* in the dictionary, you might find something like this: "someone or something having power, authority, or influence; a master or ruler." Humanly speaking, you might have several "lords" in your life, but when it comes to the Lordship of Jesus Christ, it is truly all or nothing.

Perhaps you recall the very first of God's Ten Commandments? In Exodus 20:2, we read, "I am the Lord your God, Who rescued you from the land of Egypt, the place of your slavery. You must not have *any other God but Me*" (Italics supplied). You may find some ambiguity in that commandment, but I sure don't. I recall words I heard from Zig Ziglar. He said something to the effect that whenever he heard people say they tried to read the Bible, but they just did not understand it, he often wondered if it was the parts they *did* understand that bothered them. He then added, "Did you ever notice God did not call them 'the Ten Suggestions?'"

You, like so many of us, likely have a few favorite verses of Scripture that you have committed to memory and that you try to apply to your life on a regular basis. One of my favorites is the key text for this chapter, Galatians 2:20, which reads, "For I have been crucified with Christ, therefore I no longer live. And the life I now live I live by faith in the Son of God Who loved me and gave Himself for me." To be honest, I have days when that verse is totally in operation, and I strive to do nothing of my own desire or intent. On those days, I joyfully recall Proverbs 3:5–6. "Trust in the Lord with all your heart and lean not on your own understanding. In all your ways acknowledge the Lord, and He shall direct your pathways." Other days, well not so much. Some days, I sing, "I surrender all," and other days, it's "I surrender some." On my good days, I sing, "Have Thine Own Way, Lord," but other days, I find myself singing, "I'll have My own way, Lord." Realizing I am not alone in this regard is not much comfort.

In addition to reading the Bible, I have also learned much from reading the work of Christian authors. Some of my favorites are Max Lucado, Eric Metaxas, and Ellen G. White. Of all the Christian books I have read, perhaps none has impacted me more than *The Bait of Satan* by John Bevere. I wholeheartedly recommend you get your own copy and read it—after you finish this one, of course ☺. Mr. Bevere elaborates on the text I cited above: Galatians 2:20. He explains the importance of full and voluntary surrender to the will of God. By the way, submission that is not freely given is not submission at all. (I think I wrote about that in *PLAY NICE in Your Sandbox at Home*—just saying). I've heard someone say that forced obedience creates the heart of a rebel, and that is not at all what God wants from His children.

God wants us to yield to Him from love and appreciation for all He has done for us. He sent His Son to die that we might live. We are, therefore, to die to self so that He might live in and through us. You can pretty well expect that whatever God wants, His and your enemy wants the exact opposite. Therefore, the bait of satan, which Mr. Bevere details, is that we take back our voluntary submission and insist on having life on our own terms. As a dead man, I willingly gave up all my rights in subjection to His. The bait of satan is to tempt me to take those rights back.

Another of my favorite authors is Larry Crabb. In his book *Men and Women, Enjoying the Differences,* he asserts that at the root of any sin you can think of is self-centeredness. I did not believe him at first but have yet to prove him wrong. Think of any sin, and trace it back to its foundation, and I think you'll find yourself in agreement as well. There is only room for one Lord in each person's life. It's either Christ or self. To me, it's a no-brainer which one I should choose, but you'll have to decide for yourself. All I know is that if our churches were filled with people who sought God's will over and above their own, we would see a whole lot less conflict going on. Did I just hear you say amen?

One final thought. In case you wonder if Jesus is worthy of being the Lord of your life, consider this. At a Collingsworth Family concert, Phil Collingsworth said that all of humanity is marked by this one individual. We call the years before His birth BC–Before Christ, and the years after His birth AD–After Deity. Linguistically, he is not correct, but I sure like the thought.

CHAPTER CHALLENGE: Take a few moments to search for the poem "Dying to Self" by Bill Britton. I'll warn you it's pretty powerful, and unattainable in your own strength. But with the power of the indwelling Holy Spirit, it might just make a radical change in how you live your life.

Also, if you like to sing Bible verses, try singing the words of Proverbs 3:5–6 to the tune of "Seek Ye First the Kingdom of God" (Matthew 6:33). Come to think of it, that's another excellent verse to commit to memory and regular practice.

EXTRA CREDIT BIBLE TEXTS:

James 4:7–10

Hebrews 4:15–16

James 1:5–8

CHAPTER Y1:

God's Antidote to Self-Centeredness

Key text: Matthew 20:28: "For even the Son of Man came not to be served but to serve others and to give His life for many."

Quote*: "No one is useless in this world who lightens the burdens of another."*
—Charles Dickens

*I*n my Bible, Matthew 25:31–46 appears in red letters. To me, that means you should pay particular attention as they represent words spoken by the Lord Jesus Christ. In this portion of Scripture Jesus tells a parable about people appearing for their final judgment. Some come away happy, while others not so much. The determining factor is what they did for others, how they served others, how they met people's needs. You may find this similar to the warning found in James 2:13: "There will be no mercy for those who have not shown mercy to others. But if you have been merciful, God will be merciful when he judges you."

I find several possible reasons for why Christ may have shared this story with His disciples of that time and with His followers of today. Of the several, one is for the benefit of the "receivers," while the others are for the benefit of the "givers."

The one benefit which is for the sake of the receivers is that this could be a model for a global welfare program. I have not yet gotten political in this book, and I don't intend to start now. I think most would agree, however, that before the Great Depression and Franklin Roosevelt's "New Deal," the Church led the way in helping the poor and needy. That role has now been mostly though certainly not entirely abdicated to the government. Franklin Graham said of the victims of a Florida hurricane that if every church in the Southeast would adopt ten families, all would be properly cared for. God cares for each and every human being whether they believe in Him or not, and He expects those of us who do believe in Him, who are called by His Name, to also care for others.

Care for others, or servanthood, is one clear-cut way for you to follow in Christ's footsteps (see Philippians 2:5–13). As you serve others, God is working to develop within you a Christlike character so that over time, your sincere heartfelt desire will be to help others as Christ did—by encouraging, feeding, comforting, etc. Self-centeredness is the antipathy of Christlikeness, and servanthood is marvelous protection against this becoming your condition.

Another benefit you receive by serving or doing good to others is that it protects you from judging. As we looked at elsewhere in this book, there is a place to judge behavior that is blatantly contrary to God's Word. But having a servant's mindset will guard you against judging someone's character. When you look upon those in need as folks God wants to bless through you, then you are bound to see them in a different and nonjudgmental light.

Ideally, you have discovered there is joy in serving others, in doing to the least of Christ's brethren, so to speak, without thought of payback, reward, or recognition. Again, while serving others is beneficial for those who receive, I believe it is even better for those who give. As you read in Galatians 6:9–10, "So let's not get tired of doing what is good. At just the right time we will reap a harvest of blessing if we don't give up. Therefore, whenever we have the opportunity, we should do good to everyone-especially to those in the family of faith."

Think for a moment about significant figures in history who you admire. For many people, the answers to that challenge would include Mother Teresa, Martin Luther King, Jr., Nelson Mandela, Mahatma Gandhi. While they ministered in different parts of the world, all shared a deeply held desire; some might say a need to better humanity through servanthood. I like the quote attributed to Martin Luther King, Jr.: "Life's most persistent and urgent question is 'What are you doing for others?'"

I heard a story about Mahatma Gandhi, that as he was boarding a train that was leaving the station, he lost one of his shoes. Without hesitation, he quickly reached down, removed the other, and tossed it out of the train. When asked why he did that, he replied, "Now whoever finds my first shoe will have a pair." Wow, what a mindset. Can you imagine what a church, your church, would be like if every member or even just the majority of members had that attitude, that life is not all about them, but instead what they can do for others?

To the world, or the unconverted, the story of Gandhi's generosity would be considered foolish and totally foreign to a satisfying life. But to Him Who said, "Do to others as you would like them to do to you" (Luke 6:31), it makes total sense. And, as the Apostle Paul put it, "He (Christ) died for everyone so that those who receive his new life will no longer live for themselves. Instead, they will live for Christ, who died and was raised for them" (2 Corinthians 5:15).

My friend Jay Stoekl shared a story with me about a time when he saw someone in need, and he graciously gave her $20.00. He later saw a member of his ministry team sit with the person, get to know her, and share God's love with her. Jay relates that he gave to the person from his increase, but his friend gave of herself. Please do not discount Jay's gift or the point of the story. There are times when meeting someone's financial needs is just what God would have you do. There likely will be times when you are in a position to meet others' needs, and you won't want to let them slip by without doing what you can do.

It might be helpful to keep in mind the words found in Hebrews 13:14–16: "For this world is not our permanent home; we are looking forward to a home yet to come. Therefore, let us offer through Jesus a continual sacrifice of praise to God, proclaiming our allegiance to His Name. And don't forget to do good and to share with those in need. These are the sacrifices that please God." Such sacrifice and service seem to me to be an excellent protection against conflict in a church. What say you?

CHAPTER CHALLENGE: Prayerfully ask God to give you a servant's heart. Ask your pastor or church leaders what needs they see that you might help to meet. Consider asking others to join you to add to your efforts while always depending upon God to multiply them.

EXTRA CREDIT BIBLE TEXTS:

Galatians 6:4–5

Matthew 5:46–48

Titus 3:14

2 Corinthians 13:11

1 Corinthians 10:24

Matthew 25:40

Galatians 5:13–15

1 John 3:16–19

Proverbs 3:27–30

CHAPTER Y2:

A Blessing and a Privilege

Key text: Titus 3:14: "Our people must learn to do good by meeting the urgent needs of others; then they will not be unproductive."

Quote: *"In order to 'be a light' we need to 'plug into' The Light!"*
— Evinda Lepins

I like to read the sayings on the tags of my daily teabags. One read, "When the little me has recognized the big me, and the little I has recognized the big I, oneness is achieved." I'm still trying to figure out what that means. What I do know is that "I serve a Risen Savior, He's in the world today, I know that He is living, whatever man may say." I also have a pretty clear understanding of how He wants me to treat my fellow citizens. How do I know you might ask? Sing with me "The Bible tells me so."

I also have it on solid Biblical authority that God does not want me to keep to myself the Good News of salvation through Jesus Christ.

He expects me to share it with others. In the text known as "the Great Commission," Jesus told His followers to "Go and make disciples of all nations, baptizing them in the Name of the Father and the Son and the Holy Spirit." He went on to add, "Teach these new disciples to obey all the commands I have given you. And be sure of this: I am with you always, even to the end of the age."

I chose to include this chapter because when God's people stop looking outward, they frequently turn inward, often with negative results. Most Christians would agree as believers we should often share our faith with others. We should be ever ready to witness about our Lord and Savior and to tell of the beautiful things He has done for us individually and collectively. If members of a church family are actively engaged in such activities, they won't have the time or desire to get upset with each other. It is virtually impossible for them to have negative feelings for, or hostile interactions with, others who are striving together with them to serve the Lord. The joy and exuberance they would experience would help them overlook occasional slights from others. Little things would pale in comparison to the wonder of cooperating with God's plan for the saving of humanity.

So, if witnessing for Christ carries such blessings, why are so many reluctant to do so? Of course, there are numerous possible reasons, but most could fall under the umbrella of fear.

Some might fear they must be judge and jury rather than a witness. They feel they are responsible for decisions others may or may not make as a result of their testimony. Back in my probation officer days, I was often called to court to testify about one of my clients. Though I found that to be an uncomfortable experience at times, I knew that all I had to do was tell the truth, the whole truth, and nothing but the truth. I was not in control of the outcome; I could only share what I knew. This realization took a lot of pressure off me.

May I suggest that when you are tempted to share your faith with someone, you do so without regard to how they will receive what you share. You are not the Holy Spirit. It is His job to soften hearts and to impress us to do His bidding.

Another common fear is that we might not witness correctly, that somehow we will do more harm than good. The reason this fear is so common is that it is a lie from our common enemy who will do anything he can to dissuade us from telling people the Good News about life in Christ. You might want to pay attention to timing and what is going on in an individual's life before you witness to them, but other than that, I would not be concerned that you might do it wrong. As a witness, all you are doing is telling what you know. I think it would take more effort to do that wrongly than to do it correctly.

Some hesitate to witness for fear they don't know the Bible well enough. Again, as a witness, you need not have a degree from a seminary or a Bible college. Ask for and claim the promise found in Luke 12:12: "For the Holy Spirit will teach you at that time what needs to be said." Yes, it would probably be helpful to know John 3:16, and perhaps a few other key verses, but beyond that, you do not need to have a firm grasp of the Scriptures to tell people what Christ has done for you and what He wants to do for them. Bible study can come later once the person has expressed an interest in knowing more. At that stage, you can call on your pastor or other church leaders to help in areas you may feel inadequate.

Fourth on my list of fears that prevent God's children from speaking to others on His behalf is that they might be rejected or branded as a "Bible thumper" or some such. Oh no! You mean people might not like me because I love Jesus? You mean I might suffer ridicule? Okay, forgive my sarcasm, please, but come on. With all that Christ has done for you, should your fears of rejection or ridicule matter at all?

I'll never forget an episode that happened as I was learning about Jesus for the first time. My friend Bob, who had witnessed to me, was sharing with another friend when the friend said, "Oh come on, Bob. Isn't Jesus just a crutch for you?"

To my amazement, and at that time bewilderment, Bob replied, "No way. Christ is not my crutch; he's my wheelchair!" That is so good; you have my permission to share it whenever and with whomever you like.

Witnessing, for the Christ follower, is not optional. It goes with the territory as they say. The Apostle Peter told you plainly that if someone asks you about your hope as a believer, you should always be ready to explain it. He goes on to say that some might indeed "speak against you." He then states emphatically that it is better to "suffer for doing good if that is what God wants than to suffer for doing wrong!" (See 1 Peter 3:13–17.)

The Apostle James did not mince words when he wrote, "So get rid of all the filth and evil in your lives, and humbly accept the word God has planted in your hearts, for it has the power to save your souls. But don't just listen to God's word. You must do what it says. Otherwise, you are only fooling yourselves."

You might also want to check out what he wrote in James 1:5–8: "If you need wisdom, ask our generous God, and he will give it to you. He will not rebuke you for asking. But when you ask him, be sure that your faith is in God alone. Do not waver, for a person with divided loyalty is as unsettled as a wave of the sea that is blown and tossed by the wind. Such people should not expect to receive anything from the Lord. Their loyalty is divided between God and the world, and they are unstable in everything they do." If you feel you lack sufficient wisdom to witness for God, He just told you how to get what you need. For that matter, whatever you think might be keeping you back from being a regular and faithful witness, go to the Lord and ask Him to meet your need (see Matthew 6:33).

In his 1933 inaugural address, Franklin Delano Roosevelt gave his most famous quote: "We have nothing to fear but fear itself." Doesn't that seem to apply to Christian witnessing? And, again, if members of a church fail to engage in doing what God would have them do, they will experience unrest in their spirit. That unrest will not stay within them for long, and soon enough, it will be directed toward others, often with hostility. If this occurrence is widespread, the Church is in for some difficult times. On the flip side of that scenario is that a church where the majority of the members are living their faith and expressing it in regular witness, then—why don't you finish that sentence.

CHAPTER CHALLENGE: Find a short pamphlet or Bible tract that you like that you can carry with you to hand out to people you encounter in your day. In addition to John 3:16, memorize John 10:10 or any number of other verses that tell people they should give Jesus some serious consideration.

Do a search for the poem titled "The Parable of the Cracked Pot." I believe it will encourage you that God can use any who are willing to serve and witness for Him.

And, finally, tell your pastor or church leadership that you would like to be more involved in witnessing. I'm confident they will welcome that news and will do what they can to help you.

EXTRA CREDIT BIBLE TEXTS:

Matthew 4:19
Matthew 5:16
Matthew 9:37–38
Matthew 24:14
Mark 16:15–16
Acts 1:8
Acts 5:42
Romans 1:16
Romans 10:15
1 Corinthians 9:22–23
1 Corinthians 10:31–33

2 Corinthians 5:16–21
Ephesians 5:15–17
2 Timothy 1:8
2 Peter 3:9

CHAPTER Y3:

A Competition? Heavens NO!

Key texts: 2 Timothy 2:24: "A servant of the Lord must not quarrel but must be kind to everyone, be able to teach, and be patient with difficult people." Hebrews 13:17: "Obey your spiritual leaders, and do what they say. Their work is to watch over your souls, and they are accountable to God. Give them reason to do this with joy and not with sorrow. That would certainly not be for your benefit."

Quote: *"Most believers learn passively from clergy. However, no matter how good and uplifting this person's teaching, as long as the members are not actively ministering and speaking Christ themselves, growth lacks."*

—Henry Hon

When you think of rivalries in American culture, what comes to mind? Some might say male–female, or RedSox–Yankees. Others might say Republicans and Democrats or perhaps cats and dogs.

I dare say there is a far-too-frequent rivalry in our culture that should never occur. The rivalry to which I refer is clergy vs. laity or vice versa. Whatever your thoughts might be in this area, I hope we can agree that God is not pleased when His people work against, rather than for and with each other—amen?

In preparation for writing this book, I solicited stories about times when God's people have not represented Him very well, times when "Christians" did not act in a very "Christlike manner." Of the many I received, some were from laypeople that related disappointing tales of alleged misconduct from their pastor. Would it surprise you to learn that several were from pastors detailing ungodly behavior from their church members?

Here are just a couple of examples:

I received a note from a woman who had served as treasurer for her church for some years until a new pastor came in to lead the church. Shortly after the new pastor arrived, she received a rather formal letter in the mail, "inviting" her to a mandatory meeting scheduled just a few days away. When she got to the meeting, she found other board members present, most of whom she considered to be her close friends. She was informed that she was being removed as treasurer and that she was to immediately turn over any possessions of the church that she might have. Why you may ask was she terminated from her position? She later learned that the pastor didn't trust women to serve in prominent positions in the church.

A pastor friend wrote about a time when a church member asked him for approval to teach a class on material he felt God had given him to teach. The pastor looked over the content and determined not only was it not biblical, but portions of it were outright heretical. The pastor had to tell the person he could not teach the class in the church. Rather than submit to the pastor's authority, the man accused him of thwarting God's purpose and calling in his life. The man went so far as to tell the pastor,

"Get thee behind me, satan!" The pastor offered to help the man study out certain portions of his class, but the man adamantly refused saying he did not need to be taught by man as God would teach him everything he needed to know!

In Section Three, I cited a story from Eileen McDargh about two people in a rowboat. The boat developed a leak to which one responded by bailing like crazy while the other stood back and said, "I'm glad that's not in my side of the boat." I repeat the story here because it sure seems to me that in a church, clergy and laity ought to be "in the same boat." They ought to be about God's business and fulfilling their separate, but equally needed roles to the best of their ability.

In Romans 12, 1 Corinthians 12, and Ephesians 4, the Apostle Paul details various gifts which the Holy Spirit dispenses to members of the Body. It is impossible that any one person will have all of the gifts, but collectively, a church body can and should. For a church to be healthy and functioning, each member must contribute his or her gift.

If you read Ephesians 4:11–13 in the King James Version (KJV), you might miss a vital point of the Christian experience. It reads, " And he gave some, apostles; and some, prophets; and some, evangelists; and some, pastors and teachers; For the perfecting of the saints, for the work of the ministry, for the edifying of the Body of Christ: Till we all come in the unity of the faith, and of the knowledge of the Son of God, unto a perfect man, unto the measure of the stature of the fullness of Christ." While I appreciate the KJV, especially for its poetic language, this verse seems to indicate that it is the role of pastors and other leaders to "do the work of the ministry."

Read the same text in almost any modern translation, including the *New* King James Version, and you'll come away with a far different understanding. It reads, "And He Himself gave some to be apostles, some prophets, some evangelists, and some pastors and teachers, **for the equipping of the saints for the work of ministry,** for the edifying of the

Body of Christ, till we all come to the unity of the faith and of the knowledge of the Son of God, to a perfect man, to the measure of the stature of the fullness of Christ" [emphasis added].

For far too long, and in far too many churches, the work of ministry and servanthood has been left up to the clergy or leadership. That is not Biblical, and such a mindset limits God from impacting this world through all of His children. I am not a mathematician, but I would guess that clergy makes up perhaps one percent of the Church. Maybe it's more, maybe less, but please explain to me how the work will get done if the rest of us sit by and watch them work.

When you have a moment, I invite you to do as I did and conduct a search for statistics on pastors. You will find that the vast majority of them report working far more than the average citizen; that they feel they are on call all the time, and that their vacations, if and when they get to take them, are typically interrupted by church matters. Most expect conflict in their church, and perhaps the most distressing statistic I saw was that only one in ten pastors will retire as a pastor. Anyone involved in ministry will be in the enemy's crosshairs—might this be especially true for your pastor?

I reached out to pastors I know and asked them what they would appreciate from the people they serve. Here are some of the answers I received:

"I would like them to fulfill their personal calling from God, for them to live a life of faithfulness and obedience to His Word."

"I would appreciate them stepping up to meet the needs of the church, for them to be willing to sweep the floors, clean the toilets, etc. to pitch in and do the things that need to be done. I want them to be the hands and feet of Jesus in all aspects."

"I want the same from my members as I want from anyone—people who listen, communicate honestly about their concerns, and who listen to mine."

"I want them to have reasonable expectations of me. People got upset with Jesus when He did or did not do as they expected. Too often, I find people do the same with pastors."

"Prayer support is Number One! It makes a difference when I know my members are bringing me to the throne of God in prayer."

Lastly, "I would like them to be so in love with Jesus that they desire to be like Him. That alone would prevent so many of the issues a pastor has to deal with in the church. So much of a pastor's life is consumed with putting out fires among the brethren."

To balance the equation, I asked laypeople what they most want, need, or expect from their pastor, and here's a sampling of what I got:

"I want them to be a good preacher. I expect them to spend meaningful time crafting impactful messages, which they deliver in an appealing manner. He or she should be a leader who has a vision for the church and the ability to guide us in that direction. He or she should use their spiritual gifts for the good of the church and rely on the laypeople to fill in those gifts they lack."

"He should be concerned about his personal walk with the Lord so he can be the shepherd of the flock that God wants him to be."

"I think the pastor needs to be more intentional about giving a call at the end of the message. They spend time bringing people to the gates of heaven, so to speak. They should take the time to help to usher them in. After they have made the offer, they should not hesitate to ask for the sale. For some people, that might be their best or perhaps only opportunity to decide to accept Christ as their Lord and Savior. As a believer, I also welcome the opportunity to respond to whatever God has put on my heart from hearing the message."

And, finally, "One characteristic I appreciate is a leader who can delegate, and once any work or ministry is delegated, they place trust that the person will come through. I value the confidence in knowing that my pastor believes in me and trusts me to head up a ministry and never really looks over my shoulder."

Two of my favorite people on the planet are Bill and Pam Farrel. They are likely best known for their book *Men are Like Waffles; Women are Like Spaghetti* (an excellent book by the way). Though that is their most famous book, they have written several others that have blessed people far and near. Bill shared a quote with me that I knew I had to include in this book. He said, "Perfection is not a good goal, for if you ever reached it, we'd have to crucify you." Please enjoy the humor in that statement, but do not miss the point. If you expect your pastor to be perfect, you will surely be disappointed. They have a calling for which they have been gifted, but they still retain full membership in the imperfect and sinful human race.

On a lighter note, Bill also said you should never bring a turkey to church because they always use fowl language—be sure to read the chapter on forgiveness after reading that one!

Though I have never served as a pastor, I hold the position in high regard, and I appreciate any who are willing to answer the call. I remember a pastor who announced he was leaving the pastoral ministry by telling the church that a pastor pleases everyone in the church. He went on to say he pleases some when he comes, some while he is there, and the rest when he leaves. I find that humorous but painfully true. Please regard your pastor as a fellow servant of God, and pray for him or her regularly. Ask God to do any correcting you feel may be necessary. If you have issues or concerns about your pastor, please take them to God first and then to the pastor. No one else needs to know—at least not until you have taken those first steps. I also invite you to consider the counsel given by the famous "Author unknown" who said, "We judge ourselves by our motives but others by their actions." I hope this will increase your ability to be gentle in your dealings with others.

I would be remiss if I did not include a thought or two about the pastor's spouse and children. There are untold horror stories of how these individuals have been treated—make that mistreated—by members of the congregation. I could go on, but I feel my blood starting to boil, so I better stop soon. Suffice to say you might want to be very careful how you treat these folks. If you feel you are acting on God's behalf, then you are probably safe. Be careful, however, that you don't listen to the voice of the enemy, who may be trying to recruit you to do his dirty work. If he can't attack the pastor directly, his next best tactic is to attack his or her family. Please don't ever comply with anything he wants you to do. 'Nuff said?

As I close this chapter, let me bring your attention to Galatians 3:28, where you'll read, "There is no longer Jew or Gentile, slave or free, male and female. For you are all one in Christ Jesus." When it comes to fulfilling the Great Commission (see Matthew 28:19–20), may I suggest there should no longer be a distinction between clergy and laity? I'm told the word *laity* comes from the Greek word "laos," which simply means "the people of God." Some might be in what we commonly call "full-time ministry" for which they typically collect a salary, but all of us should be in full-time ministry, ever on the lookout for souls to win for the Kingdom of God. So, while clergy and laity have different roles to play, each is vital, and the sooner we realize that, pull together, and extend generous amounts of grace to each other, the better off we all will be. Did I just hear another amen?

CHAPTER CHALLENGE: In many churches, October is designated as pastor appreciation month. If your church is not engaged in that practice, do what you can to get it started. Please don't limit your appreciation to just one month per year. Take a moment to send your pastor a note of gratitude and encouragement every once in a while throughout the year, and recruit others to do the same. Call your pastor now and then, and ask him or her how you can pray for them, and then pray right then and there. Just be ready to call 911 if you hear your pastor fall to the floor from shock. Too many pastors told me they rarely if ever receive such calls.

Set a time to meet with your pastor, and do as I did: ask him or her what they want, need, or expect most from you and the other members of the congregation. Ask them how you can best support them in their ministry. Search online for "The Responsibility Poem" by Charles Osgood. It is not directed toward a church, or is it? You might also want to search for the parable called "The Messiah is Among You." Please use it as a model for how you should regard and treat others (see Colossians 1:27).

Section Five:

NOW IS THE TIME FOR RECONCILIATION AND RESOLUTION

Key text: Matthew 5:23, 24: "So if you are presenting a sacrifice at the altar in the temple and you suddenly remember that someone has something against you, leave your sacrifice there at the altar. Go and be reconciled to that person. Then come and offer your sacrifice to God."

Quote: *"Emphasize reconciliation, not resolution. It is unrealistic to expect everyone to agree about everything. Reconciliation focuses on the relationship, while resolution focuses on the problem. When we focus on reconciliation, the problem loses significance and often becomes irrelevant."*

—Rick Warren

omebody once quipped, "Why put off until tomorrow that which you can put off until the next day?" I'm sure that's humorous to some, but it strikes a little too close to home for me to find it amusing. I can't say I always procrastinate, but it has occurred all too frequently in my life for as long as I can remember—usually with negative consequences. When I fail to do something I know I should do, the delay typically makes the situation worse, not better. As I have written elsewhere, the fact that I am not alone in this regard brings me little comfort.

One area in which I have frequently procrastinated is in confronting someone who has offended me, or whom I know I have somehow offended. I can think of lots of lousy excuses for putting off such conversations, but few good ones. My excuses tend to focus on matters related to me and how the interaction might impact me. Very rarely do I hesitate to confront someone based on how it might affect them. And, feelings aside, as you read in this chapter's key text, going to someone who has something against you is not optional for the Christian. I dare say the same may be said for situations where you feel someone has mistreated you. When you know what Christ would have you do, you just need to do it regardless of the anticipated outcome. Read James 4:17 if you need further convincing.

You are not responsible for how the other person will react or respond to your outreach. You are only responsible for your part. Also, be prepared that your initial attempt to reconcile might be rebuffed. The other person may need more time to accept your apology, to consider the offense you allege against them, or they may not believe you are sincere. There could be numerous explanations, but whatever the reason, just be patient, and give God time to work on their heart. Take comfort in knowing you did as God would have you do, and what more can you ask of yourself?

Confronting another person, especially if he or she is a fellow church member, might require some degree of courage, but as Dr. John Morgan, a pastor in my city, said in a sermon, "Courage is not a feeling—it's an action based on faith." When you are prompted to go and reconcile with someone, just go. Your feelings will catch up to you later.

So, to bolster your courage and your willingness to speak with the other person, I'll share some tips I believe will help bring about, though not guarantee, a positive experience. First, check your motive. Are you going for a self-serving purpose? If so, you might want to reconsider. Make this a matter of genuine prayer. Seek the Lord's guidance on what if anything you should do about the situation. If you determine your cause is for the good of your relationship with them, for their personal benefit, or for Christ's, then by all means go.

Second, depending on the situation and your relationship with the other person, it is likely a good idea to give them a heads up that you want to have a serious conversation with them. Invite them to choose the time and place for your meeting. A restaurant or other public place is often a good choice. This serves to help each person keep their voice down and to maintain a level of decorum. Also, if someone else is involved in the situation, it may be appropriate to invite them to attend—just be sure you have the first person's approval before you invite them. You might also ask the other if they would prefer to invite someone else join in for the meeting. Each situation will be different, so use your best judgment.

Once the meeting is set, take some time to prepare yourself. Expect a positive outcome and response, but prepare for otherwise since it is not all in your control. Just before the meeting, do as I describe in *PLAY NICE in Your Sandbox at Work* and "Push the Pause Button." Stop before you go in. Collect your thoughts. Determine in advance that you will maintain your composure and good intentions regardless of what the other might do. Make it a priority to maintain an attitude of respect for yourself and the other person(s). Choose to have the mindset that the problem or situation is the enemy—the other person is not. (I cover this in more detail in *PLAY NICE in Your Sandbox at Work*—send me an email at *Ron@ PlayNiceinYourSandbox.com,* and I'll send you the chapter).

Formulate a win–win attitude that the outcome must be acceptable to both parties. By the way, I mean the conventional "win–win," not the newer version of "Do it my way, and nobody gets hurt." Sorry, I couldn't resist. If you have prayed and sought God's blessing, you simply cannot go to the meeting seeking solely your own benefit.

When people are in conflict with each other, it is easy for one or both to let emotions get in the way of clear thinking and behavior. By taking some time to get yourself grounded in your thinking brain, you are far more likely to prevent your emotions from taking over. You'll also be better able to model the same for the other person. Another way to help them stay in their thinking brain is to alert them that what you have to say is sensitive and could be taken the wrong way. It is a good idea to ask them to put their "best ears" on and also to assure them of your pure motives.

As you begin the conversation, after you thank them for coming, address the matter that brought you there in as factual and nonaccusatory a manner as possible. Dr. Mike Hattabaugh, the creator of Hero Marriage, advises his marriage clients to "Put the problem on the table, and talk to the problem." Doing this, he says, helps the parties stay focused on the actual problem and to avoid personal attacks. It also helps each party identify the real root of their displeasure and what they would like to see happen differently in the future. I would add that when each party chooses to stay focused on the facts, it helps each of them to remain in their thinking brain from which they are more likely to make rational, appropriate decisions.

And, finally, while so much more could be said on the subject, you must be sure to communicate effectively. So often, conflicts arise or escalate due to miscommunication between the parties. You must be sure that when you say, "A, B, C," the other party not only hears but actually understands what you mean by "A, B, C." What I'm proposing goes by various names such as *Proactive Listening*, *The Speaker–Listener Technique* from PrepInc.com, or the *Talking Stick* as popularized by the Franklin Covey Corporation.

To put all of these in simple terms, you politely say what you have to say in clear, brief segments. After each section, you pause and invite the other to tell you in their own words what they heard you say. If understanding occurred, you add more information and repeat the feedback process. If somehow communication failed, you take another run at it. Once you feel the other understands your point of view—whether they agree with you or not—you invite them to become the speaker, and you assume the role of the listener.

Communicating in this manner does take a bit more time at first, but it saves you lots more time by avoiding misunderstandings and miscommunications, which can lead to further difficulties that will require more time, energy, and resources to address at a later date. According to *Step Up Your Teamwork* by Frank Viscuso, 10% of conflicts are due to a difference in opinion while 90% are due to a wrong tone of voice. Using this communication technique will help ensure you use the proper tone of voice.

Again, thoughts of confronting a fellow church member can certainly produce feelings of dread, anxiety, and fear. But I'm reminded of an illustration I heard concerning the evacuation of one of the World Trade Center towers on 9/11/01. People were scurrying to get down the stairs and out of the building. One person froze and became immobile. She blurted out, "I can't go down—I'm scared." A voice behind her called out, "It's okay to be scared. Do it scared!"

It is a trait of human nature that we tend to put off tasks that we deem unpleasant or objectionable in some way. To overcome this tendency, Mel Robbins came up with a technique she details in *The 5 Second Rule.* When you know you should do something you don't feel like doing, count down "Five, four, three, two, one, go!" This simple process helps you to marshal your forces to be about what you know you need to do. I have used this technique numerous times—including writing this book—and I assure you it is powerful and beneficial.

One last thought. Reconciliation may or may not result in the restoration of the previous relationship. As mentioned in the forgiveness chapter, your task is to do all you can do to atone for your wrong or to grant forgiveness whether the other seeks it or not. The damage may have been too severe for the relationship to continue—at least for now.

CHAPTER CHALLENGE: Think of someone you know you need to approach and schedule a time to speak with them. Put your feelings aside and make the call. Realize that the longer you delay and debate your decision, the less likely it will occur—five, four, three, two, one, go! If you harbor ill will or resentment toward someone you feel has offended you, follow the clear instructions laid out in Matthew 18:15–17.

EXTRA CREDIT BIBLE TEXTS:
1 Corinthians 6:1–7
2 Corinthians 5:18–21
Proverbs 25:8–10
Psalm 55:12–14
Hebrews 12:14
Romans 5:10

CHAPTER N1:

Intentional Christianity

Ket text: Proverbs 21:29 "The wicked bluff their way through, but the virtuous think before they act."

Quote: *"Creating an intentional life requires that we stop responding by emotion and start walking in the truth."*

—Angela Craig

*D*id you know that in a nationwide survey in America, 21% of atheists report they believe in God? When I heard that I began to wonder what percentage of people who claim the title "Christian" truly believe in God and their lives bear evidence of that belief? How many Christians are intentional about how they represent their Lord?

You see the word *intentional* everywhere in American society today. Web sites abound such as "intentional parenting," "intentional community," "intentional family," and, my personal favorite–"intentional chocolate." So, what exactly does "intentional" mean? Perhaps it is having a defined purpose for your life and a specific plan to carry out that purpose.

Pastor and author Rick Warren has impacted millions of people through his "Purpose Driven" books. He states, "You were made by God, for God, and until you understand that, life will never make sense."

Bertrand Russell said, "Unless you assume a God, the question of life's purpose is meaningless." The funny part of that quote is that Mr. Russell was an avowed atheist.

Proverbs 3:5–6 admonishes you to "Trust in the Lord with all your heart, do not depend on your own understanding. Seek His will in all you do, and He will show you which path to take." In Mathew 6:33, you are instructed to "Seek the Kingdom of God above all else, and live righteously, and he will give you everything you need."

It sure seems clear to me that for the Christian, his or her first intention should be to do what he or she believes God would have him or her do. As it says in 1 Corinthians 6:19–20, "Don't you realize that your body is the temple of the Holy Spirit, Who lives in you and was given to you by God? *You do not belong to yourself,* for God bought you with a high price" [emphasis added]. So you must honor God with your body." I believe you could easily substitute the word *life* for *body* in that passage.

When you find yourself in conflict with someone, please don't make the mistake of thinking it will go away on its own. Yes, that is possible in some situations, but if I were a betting man, I wouldn't give you high odds. In many if not most disputes, each party waits for the other to make the first move. Chances are that both would like to see the situation get resolved, but if neither takes the first step, they might find themselves waiting for a long, long time.

Please don't let situations fester and get too far out of hand before you determine that, by God's grace, you will do your part to make it better. There is no guarantee your efforts will be rewarded, reciprocated, or even well-received by the other party. But, please remember you are not accountable to God for what others do or don't do. You are responsible for your part of the equation. Just do what you know you should do, and leave the results up to Him.

It might help to consider life as a game of three-on-three: the world, the flesh, and the devil against the Father, the Son, and the Holy Ghost. I like to ask the Father to battle the world for me, the Son to take on the devil, and the Holy Spirit to help me overcome my flesh.

You must realize we are playing this "game" on the enemy's home turf as he wrested control from Adam way back in the Garden of Eden (see Genesis Chapter 3). While that may not seem fair, the end result has already been determined, and we win! At least as we accept the blood of Christ as the payment-in-full for our sin debt and receive God's complete pardon.

It should be obvious which side wants to see Christians in conflict with each other and which does not. Just in case you don't believe that, look at what Paul wrote as found in Romans 12:17–21: "Never pay back evil with more evil. Do things in such a way that everyone can see you are honorable. Do all that you can to live in peace with everyone. Dear friends, never take revenge. Leave that to the righteous anger of God. For the Scriptures say, "I will take revenge; I will pay them back," says the LORD. Instead, "If your enemies are hungry, feed them. If they are thirsty, give them something to drink. In doing this, you will heap burning coals of shame on their heads." Don't let evil conquer you, but conquer evil by doing good." And, I might add—conquer conflict by taking the first step toward resolution.

Robert Pierson tells of a man with a reputation for laziness who was converted to Christ. At a prayer meeting, he stood and prayed, "Use me O Lord, Use me O Lord, Use me O Lord," much to the delight of the brethren until he added "but only in an advisory capacity." While that may bring a smile to your face, please don't let it be your mindset.

CHAPTER CHALLENGE: Determine that you will take action this week to reach out to a brother or sister with whom you have a conflict and do what you need to do to begin the process of reconciliation. Perhaps invite them out for coffee.

EXTRA CREDIT BIBLE TEXTS:

James 4:13–17

James 3:13

Galatians 5:16–26

Titus 2:1–7

1 Peter 1:13–16

2 Peter 1:3–8

Hebrews 12:1–4

Proverbs 25:28

Proverbs 21:3

Proverbs 13:16

Ephesians 5:1–2

Be sure to check out the Bonus/Call to Action page at the end of this book for details on how you can enroll in a free mini-course on Relationship CPR (Conflict Prevention & Resolution)

CHAPTER N2:

Not Just Good—This Is Essential

Key text: Proverbs 28:13: "People who conceal their sins will not prosper, but if they confess and turn from them, they will receive mercy."

Quote: *"I think people would be happier if they admitted things more often. In a sense, we are all prisoners of some memory, or fear, or disappointment— we are all defined by something we can't change."*

—Simon Van Booy

everal years ago, my friends Don, Randy, and I hiked into and across a portion of the Grand Canyon. If you've ever had such an experience, you know how wonderful a hot shower feels at the end of your hike. As we got to the shower location, Randy and I proceeded to go in. Don, my ever-neat friend, decided he wanted to put some things away first, and he would come in soon. After a bit, I noticed he had come in and was in the next shower stall. In a playful mood, I reached under the stall divider and pinched him on the leg.

About 30 seconds later, I heard Don call out to Randy, and I instantly knew two things. One, it was Don's voice, and two, it was not coming from the next stall. Please don't ask me who was in the next stall—I didn't stick around to find out!

My point in relating this humorous story is that it is just one of many that remind me I should not take myself too seriously. I invite you to look back at times when you have done something embarrassing or foolish, and let them serve to remind you that even though you mess up at times, God still loves you and you need not be too hard on yourself. By the way, you might consider having a church social where members are encouraged to share their most lighthearted, embarrassing moments with each other. It's wonderful when people laugh *with* each other rather than *at* each other.

Realizing you are imperfect in and of yourself is excellent protection against pride and self-centeredness, two attitudes that will hurt your Christian experience and contribute to conflict with others. Another protection against overfocusing on yourself is to be ever ready to confess your wrongs, especially if those wrongs have hurt someone else. As you'll read in James 5:16, you are encouraged to "Confess your sins to each other and pray for each other so that you may be healed. The earnest prayer of a righteous person has great power and produces wonderful results."

Author Ellen White commented on this verse in her book *Steps to Christ*, "The apostle says: 'Confess your faults one to another, and pray for one another, that you may be healed.' James 5:16. Confess your sins to God, Who only can forgive them, *and your faults to one another.* If you have given offense to your friend or neighbor, you are to acknowledge your wrong, and it is his duty freely to forgive you. Then you are to seek the forgiveness of God, because the brother you have wounded is the property of God, and in injuring him you sinned against his Creator and Redeemer'" [emphasis added].

Face it. None of us is perfect. You and everyone you know will mess up from time to time. In 1 John 1:8 we read, "If we claim to have no sin, we are only fooling ourselves and not living in the truth." But oh how I appreciate the very next verse in 1 John 1:9: "But if we confess our sins to Him, He is faithful and just to forgive us our sins and to cleanse us from all wickedness."

So if I read the Bible correctly, we are to confess our wrongs to each other when we have offended someone, and we are to admit to God that we realize we have strayed from His will and not done what He would have us to do. Can you imagine a church where confession and Christlike humility were the norm rather than the exception? Can you see how such a culture would prevent conflict or help resolve those that might arise?

And, by the way, confession is not just a "nice" thing to do; it also has a massive impact on your overall health and wellness. Look at what King David wrote, as found in Psalm 32:3–5: "When I refused to confess my sin, my body wasted away, and I groaned all day long. Day and night your hand of discipline was heavy on me. My strength evaporated like water in the summer heat. Finally, I confessed all my sins to you and stopped trying to hide my guilt. I said to myself, 'I will confess my rebellion to the LORD.' And you forgave me! All my guilt is gone."

It is difficult if not impossible to walk in harmony with God if you refuse to confess your known sins to Him. The same may be said for your relationships with others. If you know you have wronged someone, your best option is to go to them as soon as possible and tell them you realize and regret your wrong and that you desire their forgiveness. Don't worry about their reaction or response. You are responsible for doing your part to make it right; you are not responsible for their part to forgive. Leave that up to God to convict them what they should do.

Simply put, "If you mess up, fess up and move on." I can think of no better way to begin to resolve a dispute with someone.

CHAPTER CHALLENGE: Pray the prayer that King David prayed as recorded in Psalm 139: 23–24: "Search me, O God, and know my heart; test me and know my anxious thoughts. Point out anything in me that offends you, and lead me along the path of everlasting life." Specifically, ask God to reveal to you anyone you have offended and who needs to hear a confession of your wrong. Please don't put this off and give the enemy a chance to talk you out of it. Reach out to the person today, and set a time to get together within the next few days. In the eternal view of life, you will be glad you did.

CHAPTER N3:

A Common but Needless Roadblock

Key text: 2 Timothy 1:7: "For God has not given us a spirit of fear and timidity, but of power, love, and self-discipline."

Quote: *"You can't change the past, but you can ruin the present by worrying over the future."*

—Isak Dinesen

A story is told about a man who checked into a remote lodge in Vermont intent on spending a few days of solitude with nature. Shortly after he checked in, he set out on a hike to explore the nearby surroundings. He returned about an hour later totally scraped and bruised, his clothes a tattered mess. Astonished, the innkeeper asked him what happened. He replied that he had been frightened by a small brown snake he came across in the woods. After he stopped laughing, the innkeeper informed the guest that he did not have to fear those snakes as they could not hurt him. The man replied, "If they can scare you off a 20-foot cliff, they can surely hurt you."

I've always found that story amusing, but have you ever become frightened by circumstances that you later discovered were harmless and which posed no threat to you at all? If you answered yes, you are not alone—not by a long shot. Sometime, just for fun, do an online search for "funny phobias." While you'll find some you likely recognize and understand, you'll also find many that will leave you bewildered.

I chose to include this chapter because fear can prevent you from approaching a person or situation that you need to address to resolve or prevent further conflict. Fear can also lead you to act in a very unChrist-like manner, which is totally unnecessary and inappropriate to the situation. Fear is the enemy of faith and vice versa. As an unknown source once said, "Fear knocked. Faith answered. There was nobody there."

Fear is indeed a very normal human emotion, and often it is entirely appropriate. If the aforementioned hiker had encountered a rattlesnake or grizzly bear, his fear would have been justified. If you're driving on snow and your car begins to skid . . . If your wife is coming home and you haven't done the dishes yet . . . Okay, I'm kidding on that last one but I hope you get my point that we all experience appropriate and inappropriate fear from time to time.

For the Christian, there are two distinct and separate types of fear. One you should engage in continuously, and the other you should not indulge in at all. The former is what the Bible calls "the Fear of the Lord." Do a word search in any translation for "fear of the Lord," and you will find numerous verses such as Proverbs 1:7: "Fear of the Lord is the foundation of true knowledge, but fools despise wisdom and discipline." Or check out Psalm 145:18–19, where you'll read, "The Lord is close to all who call on Him, yes to all who call on him in truth. He grants the desires of those who fear Him; He hears their cries for help and rescues them."

Solomon got really specific when he wrote "God's purpose is that people should fear Him" (see Ecclesiastes 3:15). Now please be clear—God does not mean you should fear Him as in be frightened of Him, but you should instead hold Him in high regard or reverent awe, admiration, and fear. Of course, whatever God designs for our good, our common enemy seeks to counterfeit or pervert into something else. And he has done a masterful job of getting God's people to live in fear far more than they should.

I've heard fear described as an acronym: False Evidence Appearing Real. American humorist Robert Benchley put it this way: "Anything can happen, but it usually doesn't." I have to say that as a born-again believer in the risen and soon-returning Jesus Christ, you have no good reason to give in to your fears or to let them prevent you from going to someone to seek reconciliation and resolution of whatever may have come between you and them. Such division is not of God. Read John 10:10 and see if you agree: "The thief's (or satan's) purpose is to steal, kill and destroy. My [Jesus] purpose is to give them a rich and satisfying life." Other translations say He came that we should "have life more abundantly" (KJV) or "have it to the full" (NIV).

I dare say it is difficult if not impossible to have a rich and satisfying life while harboring ill will or discontent toward another of God's children. When you know you should have a potentially uncomfortable conversation with someone, be prepared to have all sorts of thoughts enter your mind for why you should not do so. I promise that you will hear thoughts that speak loudly against going and that you should just, as they say, "let sleeping dogs lie." I can also assure you, however, that most if not all of these thoughts originate with the devil, not with God.

Fear of God is always a good determinant for behavior; fear of self or man rarely if ever is. In Luke 10:41, Jesus lovingly rebuked Martha when she lost her perspective and focused on minor issues. Always keep the big picture in mind, and do what you know God would have you do.

Do your part. Leave the results to him. Just please don't let fear or worry stop you. As the late Pastor Adrian Rogers said, "When you have a job to do, begin this very hour. You provide the will; God provides the power."

CHAPTER CHALLENGE: Abundant research proves that while it is difficult to talk yourself out of a negative or hesitant emotion, action will help turn your feelings to the positive. To borrow from Nike, for a moment, I suggest that you "Just do it!" Determine you will put your fears aside within the next seven days and reach out to the other person(s) to begin the process of reconciliation.

Also, if you are so inclined, join me on a campaign of sorts. I am so tired of hearing that a chocolate bar is "awesome," or a movie was "awesome," or, well, you get my point. If ordinary pleasures in life are "awesome," what do you have left to describe God Almighty? I say we band together and ban the use of the word to describe anything or anyone other than Him. Are you with me?

Section Six:

IDENTIFY THE REAL BASIS OF THE DISPUTE

Key text: Matthew 6:33: "Seek the Kingdom of God above all else, and live righteously, and he will give you everything you need."

Quote: *"Ignorance is the root cause of all difficulties."*

—Plato

You might be surprised that I would use an illustration from the television show *Saturday Night Live*, which is anything but a God-honoring program, at least in my humble opinion. In my BC (Before Christ) days, it was one of my favorite shows.

Gilda Radnor played a character named Emily Litella, who gave editorial replies on Chevy Chase's news broadcasts. She would go off on a tirade about some issue such as people getting upset about violins on television only to be corrected by Mr. Chase that she had misunderstood the topic at hand. He told her it was violence on TV, not violins on TV, that had people upset. Once corrected, she always replied with a high-pitched

"Never mind." These skits evoked great laughter from the audience and viewers, but in real life, similar situations play out regularly with anything but humorous outcomes.

One of my great delights during my 30+ year career as a mediator has always been to help people realize that situations that find them at odds with each other are often based on something entirely different than what each might think is the cause. For example, a wife might get upset with an expense incurred by her husband, and he might take it that she is trying to control him and his money. Her displeasure might actually have much more to do with concerns about financial security and how to provide for the children.

In a church setting, someone might voice concern about a sermon series on tithing and giving to the church. Other members could interpret this concern as he or she wants to dictate what will or will not be preached from the pulpit when the member's real interest could be what effect the messages might have on guests she invited to attend a service.

When you find yourself in a dispute with another person, it is vital that both you and they understand the true nature of whatever has come between you. Often both parties are accurate in their assessment of the situation, at least from their perspective and understanding. You have likely learned by now that it is difficult if not impossible to convince someone that he or she is wrong when they genuinely believe they are correct. Is the same possibly true about you?

In a former career, I was an independent petroleum landman. I was on an assignment in Hettinger, North Dakota, where I had spent the day researching properties for possible oil and gas lease availability. That evening, I called a woman in the Midwest and explained to her that I was calling her because I discovered that her property had been released. Her immediate and adamant reply was, "No it hasn't!"

I was a bit taken back by her response but kept my composure and informed her that I had checked the courthouse records, and I could assure her it had been released. Once again, she stuck to her guns and implied that I did not know what I was talking about. I started to get a bit perturbed but kept calm as I informed her that the release was filed in book 279 on page 457. She did not waver at all, and uncalmly told me, "No, it isn't!"

Both of us could sense the tension rising in the conversation when, fortunately, I had the presence of mind to ask her if she thought I was telling her that her property had been re-leased as in leased again. When she replied in the affirmative, I told her I meant the term released as in let go or no longer in effect, to which she replied, "Oh, that's true."

I can still chuckle over that encounter, and I am so grateful for the lesson I learned. So often conflicts get out of hand because one party thinks it is about something quite different from how the other would describe it.

I don't know of any better way to make sure all parties understand the nature of their dispute than for each to listen to the other as they give their version. It is a trait of human nature that we all want to be understood. You certainly have a right to be understood by fellow church members, but don't they also deserve the same from you?

I think the Golden Rule would serve nicely here. If you know you want the other person to understand your viewpoint, why not let them go first, and you earnestly strive to understand theirs? Invite them to share with you whatever it is that has them upset with you or about a situation. Once you do that, be sure to practice the admonition found in James 1:19: "Understand this, my dear brothers and sisters: You must all be quick to listen, slow to speak, and slow to get angry."

Your entire focus must be on understanding the other person's point of view. You may ask questions to gain clarity, but in no way should you try to convince them they are wrong and you are right. You'll have your chance to be heard later. For now, solely concentrate on them and their message. It is quite possible that once you understand them, you might find yourself in agreement, and the matter might be easily resolved. The same obviously could be true once they get a more precise understanding of you and your viewpoints. The objective here, again, is understanding not agreement. There will be time and opportunity for that to happen later.

As Dr. Stephen R. Covey, author of *The Seven Habits of Highly Effective People*, said, it is always a good habit to "keep the main thing the main thing." While that is undoubtedly true, it is also true that both parties must be on the same page as to what the main thing is. That will not occur unless the parties are willing to listen to each other.

The best scenario is for both parties to listen, but even if just one party listens well, the conflict can turn in a positive direction. Please never be in a hurry to resolve a dispute until you and the other party fully understand the issues that divide you. If you try to rush, you will likely "put a Band-Aid on a cancer" as they say.

Hopefully, for the Christian, the main thing in any situation is to honor Christ and to treat others the way He would have us treat them. Sometimes that might mean abandoning your own preferences and desires for the good of the church or others involved. Isn't there a verse somewhere that says something about turning the other cheek?

CHAPTER CHALLENGE: Realize there is a significant difference between listening and hearing. Resolve to not just hear what others say but strive to fully and lovingly understand them. Listen with both your ears and your heart. Dallas and Nancy Demmitt wrote an excellent book on the power of listening called *Can You Hear Me Now?* I wholeheartedly recommend you get a copy and read it.

Alan Greenspan, former Chairman of the Federal Reserve, is humorously quoted as having said, "I know you think you understand what you thought I said, but I'm not sure you realize that what you heard is not what I meant." Huh? Please determine you will not let that happen to you.

CHAPTER 11:

My Perception Is Reality—Isn't It?

Key text: Philippians 2:5: "You must have the same attitude that Christ Jesus had."

Quote: *"Those of noble soul will always do what is right regardless of immediate outside consequences or judgment."*

—I.E. Castellano

Several years ago, I was privileged to attend a conference at which First Lady Barbara Bush was a presenter. She had many good points to share, but one I remember on the lighter side was a story about two guys on a camping trip. One woke in the night, shook his friend, and asked him to look up and tell him what he saw. The friend related that he saw millions of stars, to which the first person asked, "And what does that tell you?"

The friend replied, "Astronomically, there are untold galaxies. Astrologically, Leo is in Saturn. Theologically, God is in control, and chronologically, it is 3 a.m." He then asked the first man, "So, what does it tell you?" to which the man replied, "You idiot, it tells me that somebody stole our tent!"

I've long been intrigued by the power of perception or the mindset with which we face life. You've heard the expression "You are what you eat." There is undoubtedly some truth in that statement, but I believe it is even more realistic that "You are what you think," or at least you will act as you think. Proverbs 23:7 in the KJV reads, "For as a man thinketh in his heart so is he." Even though this verse has often been taken out of its original context, there is still much truth in it.

It matters greatly what mindset you hold and nurture toward God, toward yourself, and toward others. Many times, conflict occurs within a church because members hold beliefs about each other that are inaccurate and more than likely inappropriate. Once you begin to harbor such thoughts, they tend to take on a life of their own. Before you know it, you are acting in ways that do not in any way indicate you are a follower of the Lord Jesus Christ.

You as an individual and the Church as a whole have a God-given function, which is twofold. One part is known as the Great Commission as found in Mathew 28:18–20: "Jesus came and told His disciples, 'I have been given all authority in and on earth. Therefore, go and make disciples of all nations, baptizing them in the Name of the Father, and the Son, and the Holy Spirit. Teach these new disciples to obey all commands I have given you. And, be sure of this: I am with you always, even to the end of the age.'"

The other part is the Great Commandment found in Mathew 22: 37–40: "Jesus replied, 'You must love the Lord your God with all your heart, all your soul, and all your mind. This is the first and greatest commandment. A second is equally important: Love your neighbor as yourself. The entire Law and all the demands of the prophets are based on these commandments.'"

Do you love God with all your heart, soul, and mind? That's a question only you can answer, but please don't be too hard on yourself. For me, the answer would have to be at some times better than at other times.

Do you love your neighbor the way Christ would have you do? Again, that's a question for your individual consideration. For me, the answer would be that at those times when I am at peace with Him, I more readily love and accept myself, and once there, I can do the same for others. But, at those times of inner turmoil and dis-ease, I find I treat others negatively.

Can you imagine how churches would thrive if the members could somehow keep these two main objectives at the forefront of their minds? What if each member perceived each other member as a brother or sister in the family of God? What if each member accepted the view espoused by George Eliot when she (her given name was Mary Anne Evans) said, "Why do we exist except to make life less difficult for others?" Or what if they followed the wisdom of Abe Lincoln, who once said, "I don't like that man. I must get to know him better." King Solomon, another pretty wise man, wrote what we find in Proverbs 12:15–16, "Fools think their own way is right, but the wise listen to others. A fool is quick-tempered, but a wise person stays calm when insulted."

When church members lose their focus, take their eyes off of Who they represent, and ignore their calling, it's easy to see how conflict can arise. In Colossians 3:1–4, you'll find excellent guidance for what and where your focus should be: "Since you have been raised to new life with Christ, set your sights on the realities of heaven, where Christ sits in the place of honor at God's right hand. Think about the things of heaven, not the things of earth. For you died to this life, and your real life is hidden with Christ in God. And when Christ, who is your life, is revealed to the whole world, you will share in all his glory."

Paul's counsel and focus found Philippians 3:13–14 could also help resolve conflicts: "No, dear brothers and sisters, I have not achieved it, but I focus on this one thing: Forgetting the past and looking forward to what lies ahead, I press on to reach the end of the race and receive the heavenly prize for which God, through Christ Jesus, is calling us."

Though I realize it is not wise to speak contrary to Scripture, I do not believe Paul ever actually forgot his past. I think he meant that he chose not to belabor the past or dwell on it as he faced his present days. As I wrote in Chapter A1, forgetting is not something you can will yourself to do. You can, however, choose to not hold on to past hurts, grievances, etc. I like how American historian Henry Brooks Adams put it: "Every man should have a fair-sized cemetery in which to bury the faults of his friends."

Members of the healthiest churches see themselves as a hospital for sick people, not a hall of fame for self-made superstars. All parking spots around a church should be marked handicap parking for each member, and guest for that matter, is indeed handicapped in some way.

When Charles Dickens wrote his famous line, "It was the best of times, it was the worst of times," he was describing life itself. Isn't it true that right now some aspects of your life are running relatively smoothly, while others could stand some improvement? I know that's true for me, and I feel confident it is for everyone you will encounter in church. Realizing that, having that mindset, should enable you to "cut them some slack" as they used to say.

The television preacher Joel Osteen puts it this way: "If somebody is rude and inconsiderate, you can almost be certain that they have some unresolved issues inside. They have some major problems, anger, resentment, or some heartache they are trying to cope with or overcome. The last thing they need is for you to make matters worse by responding angrily."

It is not my place to tell you what your mindset should be. I'll leave that to the Holy Spirit. I hope I have made the case, however, that if each member in a church were to adopt a biblical mindset toward one another, we would have far fewer conflicts to deal with, and we would be able to resolve those that do occur much quicker and with less damage.

CHAPTER CHALLENGE: Many times in the Bible, we are encouraged to choose. Perhaps the most famous is found in Joshua 24:15: "Choose this day Whom you will serve." May I suggest that when faced with a difference or dispute with a church member, you choose to honor God in all you do. Please remember Irving Berlin's adage: "Life is 10% what you make it, and 90% how you take it."

You might also find it helpful to memorize Philippians 4:8–9: "And now, dear brothers and sisters, one final thing. Fix your thoughts on what is true, and honorable, and right, and pure, and lovely, and admirable. Think about things that are excellent and worthy of praise. Keep putting into practice all you learned and received from me—everything you heard from me and saw me doing. Then the God of peace will be with you."

CHAPTER 12:

Aren't We All in This Together?

Key text: Ephesians 4:1–3: "Therefore I, a prisoner for serving the Lord, beg you to lead a life worthy of your calling, for you have been called by God. Always be humble and gentle. Be patient with each other, making allowance for each other's faults because of your love. Make every effort to keep yourselves united in the Spirit, binding yourselves together with peace."

Quote: *"It's in the shelter of each other that the people live."*

—Irish Proverb

I've been thinking about a word recently that has only one meaning but numerous applications. That word is *dysfunctional*, and again, it can be used to describe almost anything.

I found I had a dysfunctional pen as I wrote notes for this chapter. I have three dysfunctional trees in my backyard. Actually, they are dead, but "dysfunctional" somehow sounds better.

Most often, we hear the term *dysfunctional* used to describe human relations–especially families. While the word is overused at times, it is likely true that the vast majority of families are dysfunctional—at least to some extent and at various times.

I don't write this information to brighten your day, but do you know why dysfunctional families are so commonplace among us? It's because dysfunctional families are composed of dysfunctional individuals. And this is certainly not a new or just a modern-day phenomenon.

Think back with me to the very first human family where one brother killed another out of jealousy and hurt feelings. Think back to King David's family, where one brother raped his sister, among other illustrations we could cite. Eli, the high priest, had two sons whose actions were anything but high and priestly. Human history and the Bible are full of illustrations of human frailty, dysfunction, and sin among families.

Well, I have good news and bad news for you. The good news is that your church is a family. The bad news is that your church is a family. Therefore, almost by definition, your church will be dysfunctional at times. And, again, this is nothing new. In Acts 15, we read of a dispute between Paul and Barnabas over including John Mark on their next missionary journey. Verse 39 reads, "Their disagreement was so sharp that they separated." In Philippians 4:2 Paul appeals to Euodia and Syntyche to settle their disagreement, and he asks someone to intervene to help them do that.

So in your church family, you can and should expect to have disputes and disagreements at times. As you just read, that puts your church in good company. You should also realize, however, that discord in a church could be the enemy's efforts to get you off track from your God-given purpose and to make you ineffective. If I read Scripture correctly, however, as members of His Body, His Church, His family, it is simply not an option for us to do anything but treat each other in a loving, respectful, tolerant, and Christlike manner. Read the following few verses and see if you come to the same conclusion.

1 Peter 3: 8–9: "Finally, all of you should be of one mind. Sympathize with each other. Love each other as brothers and sisters. Be tenderhearted and keep a humble attitude. Don't repay evil for evil. Don't retaliate with insults when people insult you. Instead, pay them back with a blessing. That is what God has called you to do and He will grant you His blessing."

Philippians 2:1–5: "Is there any encouragement from belonging to Christ? Any comfort from his love? Any fellowship together in the Spirit? Are your hearts tender and compassionate? Then make me truly happy by agreeing wholeheartedly with each other, loving one another, and working together with one mind and purpose. Don't be selfish; don't try to impress others. Be humble, thinking of others as better than yourselves. Don't look out only for your own interests, but take an interest in others, too. You must have the same attitude that Christ Jesus had."

1 Corinthians 1:10 reads, "I appeal to you, dear brothers and sisters, by the authority of our Lord Jesus Christ, to live in harmony with each other. Let there be no divisions in the church. Rather, be of one mind, united in thought and purpose."

In view of these texts, and oh so many more (see Extra Credit Bible Texts below), can you see why I wrote in the introduction that *PLAY NICE in Your Sandbox at Church* is a book that should not have to have been written? And yet, horror stories abound about how God's people have treated each other at times. These stories make you wonder if Christians are more likely to *pray* for each other or *prey* on each other.

Christ prayed in the Lord's Prayer, "Your will be done, on earth as it is in Heaven." This cannot possibly happen unless and until the Church becomes unified. If this is so, why don't Christians always play nicely together? Of course, there are many explanations—far too many to detail in this book. I do want to point out two significant obstacles to church unity.

The first I heard from my pastor, Wayne Gayton: "Much, if not most, conflict within the church results from someone feeling spiritually superior to others, and they feel it is their Christian duty to set the others straight." He then added, "We compete on who is more spiritual and push our views on others. This could actually be a form of insecurity. Pride is a basic component in all conflict, and pride can also be born of insecurity, or inferiority, which results from comparison with others (see 2 Corinthians 5:16–21). How much better to have the mindset of John the Baptist, who said, 'He must increase, and I must decrease.'"

Another common obstacle to church unity is that too many members leave the management and running of a church to the pastor and leadership team, rather than getting involved themselves. When people are busy, they have less time to grumble and complain. As we looked at in Chapter Y2, when people stop being involved in outreach, they resort to in-reach, usually with predictably ugly results.

Gary Gibbs writes in *The New Winsome Witnessing*, "The reason churches are spiritually stagnant and immature is because the members have been staring at their own belly buttons for too long. They need to get their focus off themselves and onto the lost. As we break the bread of life to feed the spiritually starved, we stop cannibalizing our fellow church members." He goes on to add "Soul-winning solves a lot of problems." Did I just hear an amen?

One last word. Please note that being united does not and should never mean being identical. That would be antithetical to a vibrant, healthy church. I like how the Scottish missionary J.H. Oldham put it: "Differences were meant not to divide but to enrich."

Again, I'm dating myself, but Simon and Garfunkel wrote an insightful song titled "I Am a Rock," which tries to convince the world that one can live very happily alone and without anyone else. It's a myth. We really do need each other.

CHAPTER CHALLENGE: Ken Blanchard led an exercise at the 2018 No Regrets Men's conference in which he asked the participants to greet each other for 30 seconds in a totally disinterested manner. He then had us greet each other as a long-lost best friend or someone we had not seen in a while. Wow, what a difference! So how about you? How do you greet your fellow church members? The church should be a weekly opportunity for people to rejoice with each other.

Other ways to increase unity include these:

- Schedule a testimony and fellowship prayer time once per quarter.
- Make sure your social committee is active; rotate members in and out to avoid burnout and to bring in fresh ideas.
- Encourage each member to engage in Bible study, both individual and group.
- Select a nonprofit entity in your community for the church to focus on each quarter or perhaps twice per year. Each member should be encouraged to donate funds *and* contribute labor in some form to help meet the entity's needs and to build rapport among the members.

Be sure to check out the Bonus/Call to Action page at the end of this book for details on how you can enroll in a free mini-course on Relationship CPR (Conflict Prevention & Resolution)

EXTRA CREDIT BIBLE TEXTS:
Philippians 4:8–9
Psalm 133:1
Matthew 12:25
Romans 14:19
1 John 4:19–21
1 John 4:9–12
James 5:9
Jude 1:17–23
1 Corinthians 3:16–17

Galatians 6:1–3

1 Corinthians 10:16–17

1 John 2:7–11

Colossians 3:9–11

Ephesians 4:15–16

1 Peter 3:8–12

James 2:13

1 Corinthians 12:4–6; 12–21; 25–27

Ephesians 4:11–16

Proverbs 27:17

Hebrews 12:14–15

1 Peter 1:22–23

1 Thessalonians 3:12

Proverbs 15:4

Romans 15:1–7

Galatians 2:11–14

CHAPTER 13:

What Is Most Important?

Key text: 1 John 5:12: "Whoever has the Son has life; whoever does not have God's Son does not have life."

Quote: *"Things that matter most must never be at the mercy of things that matter least."*

—Johann Wolfgang von Goethe

*S*ome stories bear repeating no matter how many times they are told. I hope you'll agree that applies to the following: A very wealthy man had the means and desire to amass a museum-style collection of classic paintings from all over the world. His collection included all of the masters—Rembrandt, Picasso, Monet, and on and on. The man's only son shared his love of fine art, and the two spent many hours admiring and adding to the collection.

One day the son was drafted during a time of war, and unfortunately, he never returned. The man was devastated. His interest in art—his interest in life for that matter dropped precipitously. Some months later, he heard a knock at his front door. He opened the door to see a rather scruffy looking man holding a large package under his arm. The visitor told the man that he was a friend of his son and that he served with him in the army. At that, the man was enthusiastically welcomed into the home.

Once seated, he told the man the details about how his son had died. He said, "Your son died trying to save my life." He recounted the son's bravery in putting his own life at risk to try to get this man away from enemy fire. The son succeeded in his mission but at the cost of his own life. The visitor went on to tell the man of the many hours he had spent with the son learning of the art collection, the masterpieces the two had gathered over the years, and about how much enjoyment that had brought them.

Pointing to the package he had brought, the visitor told the man that he was an amateur artist and that out of gratitude for what the son had done, he painted a portrait of him, and he wondered if the man was willing to see it.

"Willing?" the man said incredulously. "Absolutely!" The visitor unwrapped the package and revealed a portrait that was a marvelous representation of the son. He then asked the man if he would receive it as a token of his deep appreciation.

The embrace that followed nearly crushed the life out of the visitor. The man had not felt this alive in months. He quickly cleared away whatever masterpiece hung over the main mantel in the house and proudly put up his newest piece. For the next several months, the man spent hours admiring the painting and recalling his wonderful times with his son.

Eventually, the man died of natural causes, and since he had no heirs, his will gave instructions that his collection was to be sold at auction and any funds collected given to specific charities. On the day of the auction, buyers and art connoisseurs from across the globe gathered in excited anticipation to view and perhaps purchase one of the exceptional works of art.

As the auction commenced, the auctioneer put up for first bid the portrait of the man's son. "Who will bid on this portrait of the man's son?" he asked. Bids were not forthcoming, but grumbling surely was. The people loudly protested that they did not gather to bid on amateur artwork—they wanted to see only the best of the best.

The auctioneer stood his ground and continued to solicit bids for the portrait of the son. At long last, the family gardener who had worked many years at the estate offered to buy the portrait for twenty dollars. "Twenty dollars once," the auctioneer cried, "twenty dollars twice." Finally after asking for more bids and receiving none, the auctioneer declared the item sold to the gardener for twenty dollars.

At that point, the auctioneer closed his briefcase and declared the auction was now over. Aghast and appalled, the people demanded an explanation, to which the auctioneer replied that he had been given secret instructions to offer the portrait of the son first and that whoever purchased the son was then awarded the entire collection.

Okay, so it is not a true story, but the moral sure is—whoever gets the Son gets it all. If you can remember this simple yet profound story, you will be in a perfect position to resolve disputes and differences you have with others. Because at the end of the day (man I hate that expression) is having your way what really matters considering the fact that Jesus Christ died for the person with whom you find yourself in opposition? Could you stand before your Lord and tell Him why you were justified in sticking up for your rights at the expense of someone else? Before you answer, be sure to check out 1 Corinthians 6:7b: "Why not just accept the injustice and leave it at that? Why not let yourselves be cheated?"

I'm not saying it is easy to put that verse into operation, but I dare say living a Christlike life in this world is rarely easy. Jesus told us as much as quoted in John 16:33: "I have told you all this so that you may have peace in Me. Here on earth, you will have many trials and sorrows. But take heart, because I have overcome the world."

In closing, you might also want to remember to set your priorities in alignment with the words of the Psalmist who wrote in Psalm 84:10–12, "A single day in your courts is better than a thousand anywhere else! I would rather be a gatekeeper in the house of my God than live the good life in the homes of the wicked. For the LORD God is our sun and our shield. He gives us grace and glory. The LORD will withhold no good thing from those who do what is right. O LORD of Heaven's Armies, what joy for those who trust in you."

Okay, really closing this time. I just have to direct you to James 3:17–18: "But the wisdom from above is first of all pure. It is also peace-loving, gentle at all times, and **willing to yield to others**. It is full of mercy and the fruit of good deeds. It shows no favoritism and is always sincere. And those who are peacemakers will plant seeds of peace and reap a harvest of righteousness" [emphasis supplied]. That seems pretty cut and dried to me—how about you?

CHAPTER CHALLENGE: When you find yourself at odds with a fellow church member, please pause and ask yourself what really matters in the situation. Better than ask, "What would Jesus do?" may I suggest you earnestly ask, "Jesus, what would You have me do?"

Section Seven:
CHOOSE TO REMAIN CIVIL AND CHRISTLIKE

Key text: Philippians 2:1–5: "Is there any encouragement from belonging to Christ? Any comfort from his love? Any fellowship together in the Spirit? Are your hearts tender and compassionate? Then make me truly happy by agreeing wholeheartedly with each other, loving one another, and working together with one mind and purpose. Don't be selfish; don't try to impress others. Be humble, thinking of others as better than yourselves. Don't look out only for your own interests, but take an interest in others, too. You must have the same attitude that Christ Jesus had."

Quote: *"You are free to do whatever you like. You need only face the consequences."*

—Sheldon B. Kopp

n 1979, scholars and researchers got together to form the Harvard Negotiation Project. They aimed to study conflict from the sandbox to the superpowers to look for ways to help people resolve disputes productively. In 1981, two members of the team, Roger Fisher and William L. Ury came out with *Getting to Yes, How to Negotiate Agreement Without Giving In.* In their book, they detail components of what they termed Principled Negotiation, a model I highly endorse for anyone who seeks to resolve a dispute with another. Their research revealed two prevalent styles of addressing conflict–hard and soft negotiation.

Hard negotiators will stay with a disagreement until they get what they want, while soft negotiators will give up whatever it takes to resolve and be done with the matter. Both hard and soft negotiators typically find success through their strategy, but at a cost. Each will make an enemy in the process.

The hard negotiator is so focused on his or her objective that they will stop at nothing until the other side complies with their demands. Thus, they achieve success, but good luck to them the next time they have to negotiate with that person, for they have turned them into an enemy through their hard-negotiating tactics. The soft negotiator hates conflict so much that they give little or no consideration to their own preferences. They reach an agreement, but shortly thereafter the soft negotiator is likely to have post-decision regret and might beat themselves up mentally for their decision.

Principled Negotiation is neither hard nor soft. With all due respect to Goldilocks, it is just right. People who adopt this style of dealing with conflict will strike the proper balance between watching out for their own interests and for those of the other party. As Christians, should not this be the standard for us in every conflict situation? Look again at the key text for this chapter, and remember the Apostle Paul's admonition when he wrote, "Don't look out only for your own interests, but take an interest in others, too." If both parties adopt this mindset, their dealings with each other should go smoothly. Unfortunately, as you have likely already discovered, this is not always the case.

So, what do you do if you want to negotiate in a biblical manner, but the other refuses to do so? Of course, the answer will depend in large part on the specifics of the dispute, but I feel safe in recommending that you choose to hold to your standard no matter what the other does or does not do.

You've likely heard and perhaps used the expression, "You make me so mad!" Really? Do others have that much control over you that they can dictate how you will feel? Yes, I realize others can get "on your nerves" or "under your skin," but aren't you ultimately in charge of, and responsible for, your response? In case you're tempted to think otherwise, I suggest you consider 2 Timothy 1:7: "For God has not given us a spirit of fear and timidity, but of power, love, and *self-discipline*" [emphasis added].

Back in the late '60s and early '70s, comedian Flip Wilson made people laugh by having his character Geraldine say with emphasis, "The devil made me do it." It was funny when he said it, but I wouldn't recommend you try that tactic. You are responsible for your words, actions, and deeds regardless of what others may or may not do. My strong recommendation to help you resolve a conflict is to choose to remain civil and to demonstrate a Christlike demeanor.

Romans 8:28 reads, "And we know that God causes everything to work together for the good of those who love God and are called according to His purpose for them." I believe that is true, but I also realize this is the end result, and it may not look like it is occurring each step along the way. Hold on to your faith and your belief in the ultimate truth of that verse; be patient and willing to operate in God's timing, and I'm confident you'll be glad you did.

One last thought. As I mentioned above, your best intentions and efforts may be greeted with scorn, disdain, and bitterness. Please do all you can to not take this personally as it likely has less to do with you than it does with the other person and what is going on in their life at the moment.

Dr. Mark Goulston, the author of *Just Listen,* and *Talking to Crazy,* has developed a thought-provoking concept that when people verbally attack one another, what they are actually doing is defending themselves from perceived attacks from the other. If true, and I believe it often is, if either party will dramatically stop the attack, the other can stop defending, and a productive conversation may ensue.

The next time you feel you are being attacked, pause and ask the person if he or she felt somehow attacked by you. Ken Futch, author of *Give it Your Best Shot*, suggests you say, "That sounded like an insult—did you mean it that way?" By asking such a question in a calm, nonthreatening manner, you are very likely going to receive a friendly response, and your conflict may just be on its way to the dispute graveyard where it probably belongs.

CHAPTER CHALLENGE: Commit Philippians 2:4 to memory. When you find yourself on the receiving end of unChristlike treatment, offer a silent prayer for divine intervention to help you focus more on the other person and their needs and wants than on your own. Rather than react to the attack, seek ways to minister to their pain.

CHAPTER C1:

Principle or Application?

Key text: Luke 6:36–37: "You must be compassionate, just as your Father is compassionate. Do not judge others, and you will not be judged. Do not condemn others, or it will all come back against you. Forgive others, and you will be forgiven."

Quote: *"What a pity human beings can't exchange problems. Everyone knows exactly how to solve the other fellow's."*

—Olin Miller

Several years ago (last millennium, in fact), I moved from my home state of Rhode Island to work at the Ski Apache ski area in Ruidoso, New Mexico. During my second year there, I rented a room from a female friend. It was just the two of us in a totally platonic, landlord–tenant relationship. After a few months, she came to me and asked if I would mind having someone else move into a vacant spare bedroom.

There was a young man (early 20s) in the community who experienced a recent loss of family members, and she wanted to extend a helping hand to him. I told her I had no objections, and I graciously welcomed him to the house. He appreciated my gesture and thanked me for my kindness.

About one month later, my friend informed me that she planned to travel in the summer and would need me to watch over her place for her. I told her I could not commit to that as I hoped to travel also. She told me she would have to find someone else, and that if they wanted the house to themselves, I would have to move out. I completely understood and accepted those terms.

A few days later, she informed me that she had found someone to watch the house and that they wanted to have it to themselves, so I would have to move out. "No problem," I said, and then I asked who she had found. Imagine my shock and displeasure when she spoke the name of our recently invited house guest.

I'm ashamed to admit that my first thought was where I should introduce his face to the pavement as I was sufficiently larger than him and could have pulled off the dastardly deed. Fortunately, reason got the best of me, and I simply packed up and moved out.

From this experience, I learned a very valuable lesson that has served me well over the years. Please don't think I am a high and holy person, but even though I was not yet a Christian, I would never have treated this person the way he treated me. To return someone's kindness with such heartlessness, I'm happy to say is not part of my makeup. I've read Dale Carnegie's *How to Win Friends and Influence People*, and trust me, it's not in there, either.

The lesson I learned is that I have no right to expect others to live by according to what I think is right. I may think they should, hope they would, believe they could, but I have no right to expect or demand that of them. We all have our personal code of ethics by which we do life and, I might add, each of us believes our code is the right and proper one for all humanity to follow. I personally don't feel that I have the right to tell others what they should believe, how they should act, etc. Even in those times when someone asks my opinion or for advice, I try to be very careful to help them discover their best answer themselves, rather than telling them what I think they should do.

I used to say I came from a family of great advice-givers. I've changed that recently to I came from a great family of advice-givers. Please read that again if you missed the difference. I could always count on members of my family of origin to share with me their wisdom on any particular challenge I may have faced. Many times of course advice from parents, older siblings, and mentors is appropriate, but all too often, advice is neither sought nor desired, and that can cause a problem.

Since churches are families, you should not be surprised when you find others trying to give you advice or telling how you should or should not deal with a particular situation. I dare say that most times, people are well motivated when they encourage you to do life according to their model or beliefs. I'm convinced, however, that far too many conflicts occur within a church because some members are trying to fill the role of the Holy Spirit for others. While I don't mean to offend you, I have it on excellent authority that neither you nor I nor any other human being is capable of being the Holy Spirit even to ourselves, let alone to anyone else.

Part of the problem is that we don't appreciate the difference between principles and applications. Principles are timeless and universal, meaning they apply to all people at all times. Here are some examples of principles:

- Prayer and communion with God are essential for a truly victorious, Christian life.
- Worship, praise, and adoration must be components of a God-honoring life.
- Obedience to God's Word is not optional for His children, etc.

There is wide diversity in how God's children apply those principles to their lives, both individually and as a church body. If you visit even just a few churches of various denominations, you will quickly see that how they pray and interact with God will vary significantly from one to another. The same is true for how they worship and show their reverence to Him. And, while most Christians would say they strive to obey God, how they carry out their obedience will, again, vary greatly.

I don't know about you, but I can say for myself that I want to be very conservative when it comes to how I relate with my Heavenly Father, His Son Jesus Christ, and the Holy Spirit. I want to be consistent and determined to do all aspects of my life in a manner that I feel God would have me do. I want to be very liberal, however, when it comes to how other people attempt to live their lives. It's a given that many, in fact, most people will hold different views on the proper way to apply God's principles. Who am I, who are you for that matter, to say that our way is the best or only way?

Without question, there are times when God calls upon His children to confront a fellow believer who is acting contrary to His will. As we read in Galatians 6:1 (among other verses), "Dear brothers and sisters, if another believer is overcome by some sin, you who are godly (or spiritual) should gently and humbly help that person back onto the right path." The Apostle Paul goes on to add this caution: "And, be careful not to fall into the same temptation yourself."

Before you seek out a fellow brother or sister for correction, please follow the directive found in 1 John 5:16: "If you see a fellow believer sinning in a way that does not lead to death, you should pray, and God will give that person life. But there is a sin that leads to death, and I'm not saying you should pray for those who commit it." Without going into an in-depth theological interpretation of the "unpardonable sin," I dare say most of the misdeeds that you, I, or others commit would not fall into that category.

When someone tries to give you advice, please be gracious and assume that they mean well. Kindly and gently tell them you appreciate their input and that you will ask God to direct you as to whether you should follow it or not.

When you're tempted to give someone else advice, please be careful to check your motives and be sure that you have their best interest at heart. Even then, you might want to hesitate and seek God's approval. In carpentry, you hear the expression "measure twice, cut once." In this situation, may I suggest you "pray twice, act once"?

CHAPTER CHALLENGE: Set aside some time this week to pray about and investigate three to five fundamental life principles that guide your life. Consider various ways you might put these principles into action. Then think about people you know, especially those in your church, who approach life very differently than you do. As best as you are able, think about what their underlying principles might be. Please be as charitable as you can.

Be sure to check out the Bonus/Call to Action page at the end of this book for details on how you can enroll in a free mini-course on Relationship CPR (Conflict Prevention & Resolution)

CHAPTER C2:

Small in Size but Huge in Impact

Key text: Proverbs 13:3: "Those who control their tongue will have a long life; opening your mouth can ruin everything."

Quote: *"Talk with your mind before you talk with your tongue."*

—Anonymous

A well-known study conducted in the 1970s determined that words are only 7% of verbal communication. The remaining components are body language (55%) and tone of voice (38%). While this study is often cited and accepted as authoritative, I sure wish someone would redo the research and see if they get the same results. My hunch is that body language and tone would still score high, but the impact of words would rise significantly. As a child, you were likely taught that "Sticks and stones may break my bones, but words will never hurt me." Does that supposed truism ever cause you to question other bits of wisdom you heard from your elders?

Even a cursory exploration of the Bible will reveal that God's people are cautioned repeatedly to be very careful with the words they use and the power of the tongue. The Apostle James did not mince words when he proclaimed in Chapter 1, verse 26, "If you claim to be religious but don't control your tongue, you are fooling yourself, and your religion is worthless." I doubt anyone ever accused King Solomon of being politically correct. He put it this way in Proverbs 15:28: "The heart of the godly thinks carefully before speaking; the mouth of the wicked overflows with evil words."

I've had the privilege of portraying the Apostle Peter a couple of times in a local version of the Passion Play titled *He's Alive*. Though I've been cast in various roles over the years, Peter has always been my favorite. That may be because I all too often relate with him, and I'm not referring to his commendable qualities when I say that. Peter is the only person I know of in the Bible who you know what he is thinking before he does because he would often blurt out words and then think perhaps he should have not said what he did.

Following his denial and reconciliation with Christ, Peter penned these words: "For the Scriptures say, 'If you want to enjoy life and see many happy days, keep your tongue from speaking evil and your lips from telling lies. Turn away from evil and do good. Search for peace, and work to maintain it. The eyes of the LORD watch over those who do right, and His ears are open to their prayers. But the LORD turns His face against those who do evil.'" 1 Peter 3:10–12. By the way, Peter was quoting these words from David's Psalm found in Chapter 34, verses 11–14. Can we agree that David was also very familiar with how the wrong use of the tongue can cause a heap of trouble?

Please note there is nothing inherently wrong with your tongue. God gave it to you, and it is vital for healthy living. But, like so many of God's gifts, the tongue can be used for good or evil. Referring to the tongue, the Apostle James wrote in 3:9–10, "Sometimes it praises our Lord and Father, and sometimes it curses those who have been made in the image of God. And so blessing and cursing come pouring out of the same mouth. Surely, my brothers and sisters, this is not right!"

We've looked at the bad use of the tongue and the problems it can cause. Here come some texts that emphasize the blessings that can accompany a proper use. Solomon instructs us, "A gentle answer deflects anger, but harsh words make tempers flare. The tongue of the wise makes knowledge appealing, but the mouth of a fool belches out foolishness" (Proverbs 15:1–2). He also said, "Timely advice is lovely, like golden apples in a silver basket. To one who listens, valid criticism is like a gold earring or other gold jewelry." Please note he said **timely advice.** As I wrote about in Chapter L3, sometimes the best advice you can give is no advice at all. That may be what the Spirit had in mind when He impressed James to write, "Understand this, my dear brothers and sisters: You must all be quick to listen, slow to speak, and slow to get angry. Human anger does not produce the righteousness God desires" (James 1:19–20).

So take a guess how many conflicts in churches have occurred because one or more members did not use their tongues in a God-honoring manner. Obviously none of us knows. I doubt even God knows for he doesn't keep score. Suffice to say the answer would be in the hundreds of thousands, if not millions. If you are to prevent or resolve conflict within your church, you simply must be careful about the choice and timing of your words. As someone once said, "You can't unring a bell," and I might add it is often very difficult, if not outright impossible to take back words said in anger, pain, or frustration. (I wrote about the benefits of calling a time-out and one essential component to make it effective in *PLAY NICE in Your Sandbox at Work.* Send me an e-mail to *Ron@PlayNiceinYourSandbox.com,* and I'll send you the chapter.)

George Thompson gave wise counsel when he wrote in *Verbal Judo, the Gentle Art of Persuasion*, "Never use words that rise readily to your lips, or you'll give the greatest speech you'll ever live to regret." If you find yourself in conflict with someone, please determine that you will maintain firm control over your tongue. If you are tempted to say something that will likely make the situation worse, please don't. The damage you cause could take months or years to undo if ever, this side of Heaven.

CHAPTER CHALLENGE: Take time this week to commit Colossians 4:6 to memory: "Let your conversation be gracious and attractive so that you will have the right response for everyone." You might also consider adding Ephesians 4:29: "Don't use foul or abusive language. Let everything you say be good and helpful, so that your words will be an encouragement to those who hear them." Wow, I want to attend a church where that is regularly practiced, don't you?

EXTRA CREDIT BIBLE TEXTS:

Proverbs 28:23
Proverbs 25:11–12
Proverbs 26:27–28
Proverbs 21:23–24

CHAPTER C3:

Discipline in the Church

Key text: 1 Corinthians 5:12–13: "It isn't my responsibility to judge outsiders, but it certainly is your responsibility to judge those inside the church who are sinning. God will judge those on the outside; but as the Scriptures say, 'You must remove the evil person from among you.'"

Quote: *"Nothing can be more cruel than the tenderness that consigns another to his sin. Nothing can be more compassionate than the severe rebuke that calls a brother back from the path of sin."*

—Dietrich Bonhoeffer

Should the Church be a place of strict conformity or more a loosely defined association where anything and everything is acceptable? Should there be established guidelines and consequences for those who break them? Does God expect His followers to hold to standards of behavior, or does He prefer an atmosphere similar to a social club where

141

members just pay their dues (tithe, in this case), and can do whatever and act however they please?

These are essential considerations as unknown numbers of churches have split over the best way to handle alleged misdeeds or outright sin of its members. Sides often get drawn, and ugliness quickly follows.

I've said it before, and I'll likely say it again: it is not your church; it is God's Church. And while your or others' preferences, opinions, etc. matter, they are not the ultimate determinant of what should or should not be done in the body.

Church discipline is obviously a very sensitive matter to all concerned. The Apostle Paul berated the members of the Corinthian church for putting up with someone who slept with his father's wife (see 1 Corinthians 5:1). He continued to admonish them that they should "remove this man from your fellowship" (1 Corinthians 5:2).

Again I ask, should people who claim to worship the God of Heaven look the other way at outwardly sinful behavior? Or should they micromanage members' lives to make sure they are in lockstep with the established rules and regulations? I hope you'll agree that neither extreme is right, but finding the balance is often a significant challenge. Love and God's justice should always be factors in these decisions, but there can often be a delicate balance between the two.

Secular organizations such as country clubs or civic organizations have rules, guidelines, if you will, to which members are expected to conform. Consequences for disregarding the rules are typically well defined, or left to the discretion of a governing body. Sir Alex Ferguson, regarded by many as the greatest soccer coach (or manager) of all time, said, "Once you bid farewell to discipline, you say goodbye to success." I'm confident he said this concerning the discipline needed to be successful in sports, but is it too much a leap to apply the thought to discipline in an organization or a church?

Now, you may be thinking, doesn't the Bible tell us not to judge others? Yes, it does (see Matthew 7:1–3 and Luke 6:37), but this applies to a person's motives, or intents, or other characteristics that are not observable.

Some have taken the "Thou shalt not judge" verse to mean no one has a right to consider another's behavior inappropriate or detrimental to the Body. Please remember that God disciplines those He loves, and at times the leaders of a church may be called upon to enact loving, Christ-centered discipline. A friend sent me a story about a head elder in a local church who left his wife for another woman. The pastor tried to reach out to the man to help him reconsider his actions, but the man refused to meet with him or to have anything to do with the church. A few months later, the new woman kicked the man out, and he sought to reconcile with his wife.

Over time, the couple was able to put their marriage back together, and both resumed their church attendance. The members were thrilled to have the man back, and they welcomed him with open arms. They also chose to ignore his sinful behavior. The man appreciated his welcome and interpreted it as a sign that all was forgiven, and he, therefore, sought to regain his position of leadership in the church.

The pastor, aware that the man was unrepentant over his actions, felt he should not be reinstated to church leadership until he had a chance to prove he was repentant and trustworthy in the position. The pastor voiced his concerns to other church leaders, who agreed with his opinion, at least until the man learned of it. Over the next 6–12 months, the man began to find allies in the church to fight for him and against the pastor. To make a long and ugly story short, the pastor was shortly thereafter removed from the church.

Why is it, do you suppose, that we Christians are often reluctant to as they used to say "tell it like it is?" Why do we sometimes tolerate behavior that is blatantly contrary to God's Word and His will? Yes, I realize that portions of the Bible are often left for individual interpretation, but in most regards, it is obvious and unambiguous. Could it be that we don't want to confront others because we fear we might be confronted with our own failures and shortcomings? Perhaps we don't want our sins drawn in the sand when we accuse others of theirs?

On the flip side of that question, why do some churches resort to shunning members they feel have sinned rather than confronting them or the situation? I know of some church organizations that use shunning as an official component of discipline, but while I may be wrong, I believe this is only done after the offending party has been informed of his or her "violations" and given the chance to repent. I know of many more situations where shunning is simply done in a passive-aggressive manner. In preparation for writing this book, I received more than one tale of members who chose to join another church and were after that summarily ignored by members of the original church.

I considered putting this chapter in the Embrace Conflict section because discipline, if conducted appropriately, can bring about true repentance and help a person restore and solidify their relationship with Christ. I chose to leave it here, however, because dealing with church discipline can be a challenge to one's walk with the Lord. Galatians 6:1 reads, "Dear brothers and sisters, if another believer is overcome by some sin, you who are godly should gently and humbly help that person back onto the right path." The verse goes on to caution, "And be careful not to fall into the same temptation yourself."

So, what, you may ask, are some guidelines if you feel someone in your church may be acting in a manner that deserves discipline? Well, since you asked, I'll share my personal views on the subject. Above all, you should pray first and pray often seeking God's wisdom. Depending on the organizational structure of your church, you should bring the matter to the attention of leadership. This, of course is unless the issue is personal between you and someone else, in which case you should simply follow the process outlined in Matthew 18:15–17. A principle to keep in mind whatever the circumstance is that the fewer people who know, the better it is for all concerned. When more people get involved in the situation than need to be, things can get ugly and out-of-hand in a hurry.

Once grounds for discipline have been established, however, please follow the admonition found in 1 Timothy 5:20: "Those who sin should be reprimanded in front of the whole church; this will serve as a strong warning to others."

Always keep in mind the difference between discipline and punishment. Discipline is for the sake of the receiver, while punishment is for the benefit of the giver. In the former case, the objective is always that the person will come to their spiritual senses, repent, seek forgiveness, and be restored to fellowship. When punishment is the goal, all that is needed is for the offending party to pay for what they have done and to suffer the consequences. I can think of lots of reasons God would want His people to experience discipline; I can't think of one where He would want them punished.

Church discipline must be handled well if a church is to be healthy. With that in mind, it is wise to follow Solomon's advice found in Proverbs 20:18: "Plans succeed through good counsel; don't go to war without wise advice." Please put aside the war analogy, and focus on the benefits of seeking out the thoughts of those you feel have God's gift of wisdom. I heartily recommend Peacemaker Ministries as a resource when you face a situation requiring objective, biblical advice.

One last note. Please don't feel a need to rush to address a situation in your church unless it is a genuine emergency that requires immediate action. If possible, take some time to pray and seek God's wisdom and will. You have likely found that an answer to a problem comes to you after it has simmered in your mind for a time. If it is an emergency, address it at once, but then take time to consider next steps. Put out the fire, so to speak, and then consider how to rebuild the house.

CHAPTER CHALLENGE: Find out if your church has an established proto-col for how to handle cases where members act in ways that are not God-honoring and consistent with Christ-centered living. Check out Peacemakers Ministry for helpful resources.

EXTRA CREDIT BIBLE TEXTS:

Psalm 94:12

Proverbs 3:11–12

Jeremiah 30:11

Proverbs 28:23

Section Eight:
EMBRACE CONFLICT AS OPPORTUNITY

Key Text: Romans 5:3: "We can rejoice, too, when we run into problems and trials, for we know they help us develop endurance."

Quote*: "In the middle of difficulty lies opportunity."*

—Albert Einstein

*H*umankind has always tried to control the environment. Near the end of the 20th century, a company called Space Biosphere Ventures conducted an experiment in controlled living, which they named the Biosphere. Located in Southern Arizona, this self-contained structure had everything necessary to sustain life. Well, almost everything.

While the designers had gone to great lengths to make sure conditions were just right, they overlooked at least two significant factors. One was the dynamics of human interactions. Though I am not well versed on the subject, I understand there was serious conflict among the eight inhabitants, which they were not able to resolve, and which prevented them from carrying out their assignments as a team.

This conflict might have been due, at least in part, to the lack of oxygen in the structure. The designers knew that trees give off oxygen, so they planted several trees, which they thought would meet the need. Unfortunately, the trees died and thus were not able to provide the necessary life-sustaining oxygen. And why, you might ask, did the trees die? It wasn't due to a lack of expertise, care, or nurture. They were watered regularly and given everything they needed—except for conflict.

In nature, trees face conflict regularly in the form of winds buffeting them side to side. In response, trees put down roots to enable them to grow stronger and to withstand the forces of nature. The stronger the wind (or conflict, if you will), the deeper the roots; the deeper the roots, the stronger and healthier the tree. In the Biosphere, there was no wind. The trees had life pretty easy and conflict-free. Therefore, they felt no need or desire to put down roots, which ultimately led to their demise. Trees need to put down roots for them to thrive and survive.

If you or I were God, we might be tempted to design a world devoid of problems and conflict. I don't know about you, but I sure am glad I'm not God. In our fallen state, conflict serves a great purpose to help us do life God's way and to prepare us for the time and place when conflict will indeed become a relic of the past.

For now, however, much like trees, we need difficulties, adversities, and yes, even conflict at times, to help develop our character and to strengthen us against attacks from the evil one. Conflict, if handled correctly, can help us grow in various ways:

- Conflict can cause us to turn to God for guidance, wisdom, deliverance, etc.
- When we face conflict, we are reminded of our need for God and our total dependence upon Him.

- Conflict can and should strengthen our hatred of sin and our resolve to turn from it.
- Conflict can lead to self-reflection to see what we may have done, or neglected to do, which helped to create the conflict.
- Conflict, when handled well, can strengthen relationships and deepen ties with others.

In Philippians 4:13, we read the well-known and often misapplied verse, "For I can do all things through Christ Who gives me strength." If you just read that verse alone, you might get the impression that you are invincible and that with Christ working in you, nothing is too difficult for you to accomplish. Before you come to that conclusion, you might want to read the two verses before 4:13, for in them you'll gain context.

In verses 11 and 12, Paul describes times when he faced adversities of many kinds, conflicts undoubtedly among them, and by going through these, he realized that so long as Christ was in charge, he could endure anything that life might throw at him.

Another oft-quoted verse, which I believe is typically taken out of context, is James 1:2. In the KJV it reads, "My brethren, count it all joy when ye fall into diverse temptations." If you were to take this verse by itself, you might be tempted to jump for joy whenever you experience difficulties or hardships. You might feel you should say things like, "I just broke my leg. Man, I couldn't be happier!" Or "I just lost my job, and I don't know how I will support my family—isn't that great!"

Okay, I'm being facetious (thank God for spell check!), but isn't that what the verse seems to imply—that you should rejoice and celebrate when life brings disappointments your way? Let's look at the rendering in the NLT and add verses three and four: "Dear brothers and sisters, when troubles of any kind come your way, consider it an *opportunity for great joy* (emphasis added). For you know that when your faith is tested, your endurance has a chance to grow. So let it grow, for when your endurance is fully developed, you will be perfect and complete, needing nothing."

Conflict within a church is inevitable at times. Conflict does not mean you're in the wrong church or that there is something wrong with you or the other party with whom you disagree. Conflict, as we just read, could open the door for God to bring about His will in His Church, and He might just want to use you to accomplish His purposes.

Now, please don't go out of your way to create conflict just so you can receive (or give) a blessing, but please don't run away from it either in hopes it will go away. The chances of that happening are not good. Instead, when you face a potentially divisive situation with someone, sincerely seek God's purpose and direction in the matter. Be willing to learn and grow in whatever ways He desires for you. Also, be open to what He might want to accomplish in the other person or persons.

CHAPTER CHALLENGE: When faced with a difficult situation with a fellow believer, be open to a positive outcome. Memorize and claim the promise found in Romans 8:28: "And we know that God causes everything to work together for the good of those who love God and are called according to His purpose for them."

Remember also what we read in Hebrews 2:18. "Since He (Christ) Himself has gone through suffering and testing, He is able to help us when we are being tested."

Be sure to check out the Bonus/Call to Action page at the end of this book for details on how you can enroll in a free mini-course on Relationship CPR (Conflict Prevention & Resolution)

CHAPTER E1:

Comfort Zone

Key text: 2 Corinthians 3:16–18: "But whenever someone turns to the Lord, the veil is taken away. For the Lord is the Spirit, and wherever the Spirit of the Lord is, there is freedom. So all of us who have had that veil removed can see and reflect the Glory of the Lord. And the Lord—Who is the Spirit—makes us more and more like Him as we are changed into His glorious image."

Quote: *"Change is the law of life. And those who look only to the past or present are certain to miss the future."*

—John F. Kennedy

There's a story about a Jewish man seated on a plane when the flight attendant asked him, "Are you comfortable," to which he replied, "I have a few dollars set aside." My Jewish background helps me to see the humor in that story. I hope you can as well.

We humans are all so unique and different from one another, yet we share so many commonalities as well. One such commonality, at least among Americans, is an aversion to change. We tend to get comfortable in our ways and resent being told we must act, think, or behave differently. We don't like it when we are forced out of our "comfort zone."

Truth be told, however, we don't really dislike or seek to avoid change. As I once heard it said, "People do not resist change nearly as much as they resist being changed." You can think of times in your life when you decided to change some aspects. You decided to start or end a relationship, to end or begin your work situation, to relocate, etc. Chances are you have fond memories of those changes.

You can also likely recall times when someone told you your relationship with them was over, or your job ended for reasons outside of your choice, or you were forced to move, etc. These changes likely evoke negative, unpleasant memories. Perhaps, then, a comfort zone has more to do with being in control and dictating how life should be than with actual pleasure?

So, what does this have to do with resolving conflict in a church? Unfortunately, we have all heard of church splits over the change in the color of the carpets, the setting of the thermostat (police were called over that one), or other seemingly inconsequential matters that can become huge issues to some. A friend recently shared a story with me about a pastor who was quite tech-savvy. Unfortunately, he was assigned to a church that was, how should I say, stuck in the past? He began using his iPad and PowerPoint to illustrate his sermons. While this is a fairly common practice today, it was met with overt and hostile opposition. The members made the pastor's life miserable and accosted him with Biblical "truth" that technology is not from God! You probably won't be surprised to learn that the pastor soon left that church, and God led him to another where his talents were more appreciated.

It should come as no surprise that within our churches, we will find varying opinions about how things should be done. Our entire American society, it seems, is continuously at odds with itself over changing the way we do things (Progressives) or keeping things just as they are (Conservatives). My personal view is that there is some wisdom on both sides, but unfortunately, feelings, personalities, and biases get in the way of either side giving credence to the other. We accept this as the norm in politics, but should it be that way in God's Body, His Church?

Leadership expert John Maxwell states, "If we're growing, we're always going to be out of our comfort zone." While he intended that thought to apply to individuals, I don't think it is too far a stretch to apply it to churches as well. Surely a church that stays in its comfort zone will not be a healthy, growing church. In the big picture of life, it seems to me that a comfort zone is overrated and self-limiting. The fact remains, however, that change and discomfort, can readily bring about conflict if the parties involved do not handle it well. It's also true that getting out of one's comfort zone can often lead to growth, resolved conflict, and an overall better life.

Allow me please to stay on the subject of your comfort zone just a bit longer as I challenge you to consider what the comfort zone may have been for some biblical or historical characters. Say John the Baptist, for example, or the Apostle Paul. How about Martin Luther, Huss, or Jerome, or any of the martyrs who gave their lives for the cause of Christ? How would you describe the concept of a comfort zone to them? Let's put Jesus Himself into that challenge. I would love to hear you explain to Him why your life should be comfortable and change- or problem-free.

Please don't get me wrong; I am not advocating that life should never be comfortable. I just believe that your comfort zone should never be your goal or priority. I also think for the Christian, a comfort zone will always involve walking in harmony with Christ. If you can agree with that viewpoint, do you believe a Christian could ever be in a comfort zone at the same time he or she is upset with, or holding a grudge against, a fellow believer? Please read Mathew 5:21–24 before you answer. Can you ever see yourself telling the Lord, "I know I should go apologize to someone I have wronged, but I'm just not comfortable doing that?"

Change is happening all the time, whether you like it or not—sometimes for the better and sometimes not so much. My purpose in writing this chapter is to challenge you to take a Christlike perspective on change and to seek His will in your role either for or against the change. There likely will be times when you feel so convicted that you must take a stand one way or the other. Please just be sure that your motives are right and that you are not seeking to impose your will on others for your selfish purposes.

Sometimes the best-made plans need to change. To that point, a pastor in my area, Christie DeWeese, said, "Many of Jesus' miracles occurred while He was on His way elsewhere, but He suspended His pursuits to serve, to meet needs." As I wrote in a previous chapter, it is always a good idea to keep the main thing the main thing. To change or not should never be an end in and of itself. The "why" behind the change is what matters as well as how you go about bringing it to fruition. And, I might add, the "why" should always be centered on what you perceive to be God's will, not your own.

When I suggested you should embrace conflict in the previous chapter, I did not mean you should go out of your way to create it. The same is true when I suggest you embrace change. You don't need to look for opportunities for conflict or change—trust me, they will find you.

One final thought. There may be times when you feel things are not quite right in the church you attend. Before you decide to leave and worship elsewhere, be sure to ask God if that is what He would have you do. As one who has committed his or her life to Christ, it is no longer your decision where you worship Him. God may have a plan for that church, for which He may want and need your participation. Please keep in mind, it is His church, not yours (it seems like maybe I've said that a time or two). If you're convinced it is a change God wants, you might want to remember the words allegedly ascribed to Mahatma Gandhi: "Be the change you want to see in the world." I doubt he would mind if we substituted the word *church* for *world*, do you?

CHAPTER CHALLENGE: When someone in your church proposes a change, strive to respond with a desire to understand more, rather than to resist. Ask the person to explain not just what they request but why. Help them to clarify for you how the change will benefit them and the church family. Refrain from giving an opinion either for or against until you have had time to pray and consider the matter.

For a humorous look at change within the church, search for Cows in the Corn, Hymns vs Choruses.

CHAPTER E2:

To God Be the Glory—Stories for Hope and Encouragement

Key text: Ephesians 3:20–21: "Now all glory to God, who is able, through his mighty power at work within us, to accomplish infinitely more than we might ask or think. Glory to him in the church and in Christ Jesus through all generations forever and ever! Amen.»

Quote: *"God will always provide; it just might look different than what we had in mind."*

—Author unknown

We Christians in America have it so good compared to much of the rest of the world that we sometimes forget that Christ warned us as found in John 16:33: "Here on earth you will have many trials and sorrows." He went on to add, "But take heart because I have overcome the world."

When you face conflict with a fellow believer, or you find turmoil in your church, it is easy to conclude that God is upset with you or that He is AWOL from the situation. Please do not give in to those thoughts. As Pastor John Lindell once tweeted, "When God is going to do something wonderful, He begins with difficulty. When He is going to do something incredible, He starts with the impossible."

So, in case you find yourself in an unpleasant situation, I want to share with you some stories that I hope will give you an increased sense of encouragement and expectation. These are stories of times when God has shown up and blessed me in ways that defy human logic. I love to recount them as they serve to remind me of God's love and watchful care over me.

Years ago, I put some of these stories into a sermon that I preached a few times at various churches but never named. One day, I was on my way to share this message with some folks, and I decided to call a pastor friend since I was scheduled to preach at his church the following week. I told him what I wanted to share, and he liked the idea. He then asked me the name of the sermon, and I had to admit it did not have a title. Just then it hit me that the title should be To God Be the Glory. It was a perfect title as the stories were not about me and my goodness in any way, but about Him.

We ended our conversation, and I got two quick impressions. One was regret that I had not named the sermon earlier because I could have asked that To God Be the Glory be the opening song for the service. The second impression was, "I wonder if it will be?" I got to the church and opened the bulletin. I simultaneously laughed and cried as my eyes found the title of the opening song. Just in case you don't believe me, I still have that bulletin, which listed what for obvious reasons is now one of my absolute most favorite hymns: To God Be the Glory. The rest of the first verse reads, "Great things He has done. So Loved He the world that He gave us His Son. Who yielded His life, an atonement for sin, and opened the life gate that all may go in." Feel free to stop reading and sing the rest if you like. I just did.

Another of my favorite "God Moments" occurred when my wife and I went out to dinner one evening just because that's what married folks should do once in a while. By that, I mean it was no special event that we were celebrating—at least that's what we thought. During the meal, I had a strong impression that I should get out my calculator and figure out how many days we had been married. I counted the years and multiplied them times 365. I then went back and determined how many of those years had leap days to be added in. Finally, I counted the days since our last anniversary. Years later, I still vividly recall the thrill I experienced as I showed my wife the results on the calculator. That day that we just so happened to decide to go out for dinner, that day when I was impressed to get out my calculator to determine how many days we had been married was our 10,000th day of marriage.

As good as that story is, it gets even better. Just a few weeks later, I was invited to preach in the church in which we had gotten married those many years before. Since many in the congregation that morning had been at our wedding, I had to share that wonderful blessing with them. In attendance that morning was a couple who had gotten married precisely one week before my wife and me. When I shared the story, they decided they would go back, after the sermon, of course, to determine when their 10,000th day was and see if they could recall where they were or what they did on that day. To their great delight and amazement, they realized that on that particular day, they had been at their daughter's graduation from a small Christian college where she was given a plaque for being—are you ready for this?—the 10,000th graduate from that college. What a mighty and loving God we serve!

There are several other tales I could tell you of times when God has demonstrated His love for me over and above the basic miracle of giving me breath each day. Please realize, as I do, that I am no more special or loved than any of God's other children. I do sometimes feel like the Apostle John, who liked to refer to himself as "the disciple whom Jesus loved." Some might think he was being arrogant in claiming that title, but I don't believe that is correct. I think he just realized and appreciated his standing with Christ, which should be the same for all of us, don't you think?

CHAPTER CHALLENGE: Be on the lookout for God's working in your life—mini-miracles if you will—and record them in either written or verbal form to make sure you never forget. In the midst of conflict, it will help you to remember that God loves and cares about you—as He does for the other person(s), and that He never changes. Remember the words written in Hebrews 13:8. "Jesus Christ is the same yesterday, today, and forever."

Just for fun, ask Siri or whoever your phone assistant is how many days have passed since your date of birth. Do the same for others whose birthdate or anniversary you know, and look to celebrate milestones. I just did that and noted on my calendar to celebrate on February 20, 2020—my 25,000th day since my biological birth. Sorry you missed the party.

CHAPTER E3:

Unite and Conquer?

Key text: John 17:21: "I pray that they will all be one, just as you and I are one—as you are in me, Father, and I am in you. And may they be in us so that the world will believe you sent me."

Quote*: "Though we cannot think alike, may we not love alike? May we not be of one heart, though we are not of one opinion? Without all doubt, we may. Herein all the children of God may unite, notwithstanding these smaller differences."*

—John Wesley

God has many names, and I do not mean Yahweh, Jehovah, or others of which you may be thinking. I refer to "Art" or "Harold" as in Our Father Who *Art* in Heaven, *Harold* be Thy Name. One of my favorite names for Jesus is "Andy" taken from the hymn In the Garden–"*Andy* walks with me, *Andy* talks with me."

Okay, enough Ron-foolery. God's Church also goes by many different names. I saw an estimate recently that there are some 45,000 Christian denominations in the world. Many of these are offshoots or subsets that still closely identify with the doctrines and practices of a major denomination, rather than 45,000 distinct faiths. I find it amusing and somewhat troubling that the vast majority of these 45,000 denominations are convinced that they are biblically sound, and everyone else has somehow missed the mark. While it is certainly not my place to judge, doesn't it seem like Jesus' prayer in John 17:21 that we "all be one" has mostly gone unanswered?

Denomination is a term that has some benefits but also limitations. While a denominational name may tell outsiders what a particular congregation believes, it can also serve to divide and separate and in effect, create "outsiders." This might be a factor to explain the recent growth of community churches. Some community churches simply remove the denominational label but still adhere to the doctrines and organizational structure to which they ascribed before the name change. Others go through a divorce, if you will, from the original church and create a new independent entity.

Throughout the history of the Church, various faiths have emerged often but not always due to disagreements and conflict. Perhaps events may have been different if they had focused more on the words found in 2 Timothy 2:14: "Remind everyone about these things, and command them in God's presence to stop fighting over words. Such arguments are useless, and they can ruin those who hear them."

Other religions have developed due to the charismatic leadership of an individual or group. However they began, many of these faiths have made significant contributions to Christianity. While I do not claim to be a church historian, I thank the Baptists of yesteryear for reminding Christians of the importance of baptism. In more recent times, they have led the way in urging Christians to support and participate in missions. I credit the Assembly of God faith for bringing to our awareness the Ministry of the Holy Spirit and His essential role in living a Christian life. In the mid to late 1800s, the Seventh-day Adventist Church brought back the vital truth of the imminent second coming of our Lord Jesus Christ. They have also played a role in reminding Christ's followers, and nonbelievers, that it matters how they treat their bodies and the importance of healthful living.

Obviously, there are many more I could cite, but if I were to do so, I would invariably omit some, and that is a risk I am not willing to take. Suffice to say that today's Christianity owes a debt of gratitude for contributions made by those who have gone before us.

While denominational differences have been beneficial in some regards, there can be no doubt that they have caused problems as well. I do not have an issue with the fact that Christians have a wide variety of ways to worship their Lord and Savior. We are all alike in many respects, but oh so different in others. What one might consider an entirely appropriate way to conduct church could be an anathema (there's a proper Bible word for you) to someone else. I appreciate the quote by Priscilla Shirer, "Unity does not mean sameness. It means oneness of purpose."

I like to visit various churches from time to time; in fact, I've had the privilege to preach in a dozen or so. Each time I worship with believers, not of my own faith, I always find some aspects I appreciate and some I question. But, as I learned a long time ago, what I believe or prefer, has little relevance to what others should or should not do. I challenge you to consider taking a weekend now and then to worship with your brothers and sisters in a church other than the one you regularly attend. I cannot promise what will happen, but I can assure you of a blessing if you are willing to seek one. I find, at the very least, I come away from a different church stronger in my convictions or open to challenging some long-held beliefs. Either outcome holds benefit for my growth and development as a follower of Christ. I challenge you to be so secure in what you believe that you are never threatened by others who think differently. Also, be ever open to receiving new truth that God might want you to know. As Solomon advised in Proverbs 18:15, "Intelligent people are always ready to learn. Their ears are open for knowledge."

Differing denominations are a fact of life, and that is not likely going to change this side of Heaven. And, again, while that is not necessarily a bad situation, can you imagine how Christ feels when He sees His followers divisive, hostile, and separate from each other? Before you answer that question, please take a moment and read the next few verses of Scripture:

In 1 Corinthians 1:10, the Apostle Paul wrote, "I appeal to you, dear brothers and sisters, by the authority of our Lord Jesus Christ, to live in harmony with each other. Let there be no divisions in the church. Rather, be of one mind, united in thought and purpose."

The Apostle John gave a stern warning found in 1 John 4:7–8: "Dear friends, let us continue to love one another, for love comes from God. Anyone who loves is a child of God and knows God. But anyone who does not love does not know God, for God is love." He continues later in the same chapter, "If someone says, 'I love God,' but hates a fellow believer, that person is a liar; for if we don't love people we can see, how can we love God, whom we cannot see? And he has given us this command: Those who love God must also love their fellow believers" (1 John 4:20–21). Please note he did not limit that to only members of your congregation.

There are so many other texts I could have chosen, and in fact, I have listed several at the end of this chapter for your further review. One verse, in particular, that should give you concern is Matthew 12:25: "Jesus knew their thoughts and replied, 'Any kingdom divided by civil war is doomed. A town or family splintered by feuding will fall apart.'" Whether we like it or not, the truth is we're all in this together, and the sooner we realize that, perhaps, the sooner we can go home, don't you think?

You might also want to remember that the Church is not ours but Christ's, and He refers to the Church as His Body (see Ephesians 1:20–

23). Can you imagine what the Church—the world, for that matter—would be like if all adherents followed biblical instructions such as Ephesians 6:18: "Pray in the Spirit at all times and on every occasion. Stay alert and be persistent in your prayers for all believers everywhere." Or Colossians 3:14: "Above all, clothe yourselves with love, which binds us all together in perfect harmony." That sure sounds like a better world to me, how about you?

CHAPTER CHALLENGE: Revisit Chapter C1 Principles and Applications and consider how that information might apply to this chapter.

For a lighthearted look at denominational differences, check out Tim Hawkins' You Tube video on hand-raising.

Take some time this week to read the texts below. Consider memorizing some of them, and seek to put them into practice. Select a specific church in your community to pray for each week. Ask God to bless them abundantly.

Be sure to check out the Bonus/Call to Action page at the end of this book for details on how you can enroll in a free mini-course on Relationship CPR (Conflict Prevention & Resolution)

EXTRA CREDIT BIBLE TEXTS:

1 Peter 3:8

Romans 12:4–5

Romans 15:6

Philippians 1:27

Romans 12:16

Romans 14:19

Acts 4:32

Romans 15:5–7

Ephesians 1:10

Ephesians 4:1–32

Philippians 2:1–8

1 Corinthians 15:58

Ephesians 2:14

Titus 3:10–11

1 Corinthians 12:12–31

Romans 8:1–39

John 13:35

Romans 12:5, 10

Acts 20:28

1 John 4:11

Hebrews 10:24–25

Ephesians 5:11

Colossians 3:1–25

1 Corinthians 13:1–13

Closing Thoughts

As I said at the beginning, this is a book that should never have needed to be written. We modern-day Christians look back with disbelief at the repeated failure of the Jewish people to comply with God's directives and to walk in obedience to and connection with Him. Yet, if we are honest, can we be so confident we would not have done precisely as they did, or perhaps even worse?

And what about us today? Do you know a church, or a person for that matter, who lives in perfect harmony with God and all that He asks of us? I doubt it, simply because churches are composed of imperfect people, all of whom will be hypocrites at times. Often, people say they won't go to church because of all the hypocrites there. I always respond by saying they should not worry; there's still room for one more. Also, if you let a hypocrite come between you and God, then by definition and position, the hypocrite is closer to God than you are.

Please rest easy. Perfection is not what God asks or expects of us. In my humble, non-theologian mind, I believe all God wants from us to is "do justly, to love mercy, and to walk humbly with your God" (Micah 6:8—see various translations). What that involves is a subject for an entire book, which I will defer to a more theologically trained person than me.

Hopefully, you are convinced that God cares about you and about how you treat His other children. If I dare say so myself, He wants you to play nicely with them. I like the directive often attributed to John Wesley: "Do all the good you can. By all the means you can. In all the ways you can. In all the places you can. At all the times you can. To all the people you can. As long as ever you can."

In this book, I endeavored to give you Biblically based, useful, practical means to either prevent or resolve conflict and to treat others as you would have them treat you. In theory, that should not be difficult, but often it is a different story in practice. I invite you to set aside time each week to focus on one or two of the strategies you just read and to prayerfully consider how you might put them into operation in your life. You might consider asking others in your church to join you in that undertaking. You might also want to look into the small group study materials – see the Bonus/Call to Action page for more details

No model or system for conflict management will work in every situation. If you find yourself in a seemingly unresolvable situation, maybe you should just do as we read in Proverbs 18:18: "Flipping a coin can end arguments; it settles disputes between powerful opponents." I find most people do not like that option, but might it be better than going to court or losing a brother or sister for whom Christ died?

As I close, I thank you for reading my book, and I invite you to purchase the first two books in the series: *PLAY NICE in Your Sandbox at Work*, and *PLAY NICE in Your Sandbox at Home*. In each of these books, you'll find other helpful tips and tactics to manage conflict more productively in those areas of your life.

I also want to leave you with just a few more Bible texts that somehow did not find their way into the main body of the book. Hopefully they will confirm for you that any efforts you put into being a peacemaker will place you firmly in line with God's Will.

2 Corinthians 13:11—Dear brothers and sisters, I close my letter with these last words: Be joyful. Grow to maturity. Encourage each other. Live in harmony and peace. Then the God of love and peace will be with you.

1 Thessalonians 5:15—See that no one pays back evil for evil, but always try to do good to each other and to all people.

Ephesians 6:10—A final word: Be strong in the Lord and in his mighty power.

Colossians 3:14–17—And above all these put on love, which binds everything together in perfect harmony. And let the peace of Christ rule in your hearts, to which indeed you were called in one body. And be thankful. Let the word of Christ dwell in you richly, teaching and admonishing one another in all wisdom, singing psalms and hymns and spiritual songs, with thankfulness in your hearts to God.

Jude 1:24–25—Now all glory to God, who is able to keep you from falling away and will bring you with great joy into his glorious presence without a single fault. All glory to him who alone is God, our Savior through Jesus Christ our Lord. All glory, majesty, power, and authority are his before all time, and in the present, and beyond all time! Amen.

FINAL CHAPTER CHALLENGE: Search online for the song "Let It Be Said of Us." I believe you'll find the message to be a worthy goal for your life. It reminds me of Mark Twain's challenge: "Let us endeavor so to live that when we come to die, even the undertaker will be sorry."

Ron Price MA

Author, Speaker, Trainer, and Humorist

A: 1909 E. 20th #5
     Farmington, NM 87401

P: 505 324-6328

M: 505 330-8795

E: ron@PlayNiceinYourSandbox.com

W: www.PlayNiceinYourSandbox.com

Bonus/Call to Action

I often say that while conflict is inevitable, damaged relationships are optional.

You have likely experienced the pain of a lost or damaged relationship with a friend or a loved one. Most of us have, but what if you knew some essential tools, tips, and techniques to help you maintain vibrant, healthy relationships with the important people in your life.

While I have shared many such bits of information in this book, there are plenty more where they came from. If you enjoyed reading *PLAY NICE in Your Sandbox at Church*, I'm confident you will enjoy the free mini-course I'm offering to all readers of this book.

Would you like to know how to:

- Stop an argument in its tracks?
- Prevent people from pushing your buttons?
- Maintain control of your emotions when others are losing theirs?
- Deal with difficult people and difficult situations?

If you answered yes, send me an email to Ron@PlayNiceinYourSandbox.com. Put Free Mini-Course in the subject line and I'll send you the link.

Also, I have developed small group study materials to help you and your fellow church members learn how they can enjoy more peace and joy, with less stress and strife – at home, at work, and at church. Send me an email with Small Group Study Materials in the subject line to Ron@PlayNiceinYourSandbox.com for details.

And, lastly, I welcome the opportunity to speak to your members and/or leadership team. Let's talk about how we might make that happen - virtually or in person.

I'll close with the wonderful words of encouragement found in Ephesians 3:20, 21: Now all glory to God, who is able, through his mighty power at work within us, to accomplish infinitely more than we might ask or think. Glory to him in the church and in Christ Jesus through all generations forever and ever! Amen.

About the Author

Though he started life in the Jewish faith, Ron Price, MA, has spent the majority of his adult life as a follower of his Lord and Savior Jesus Christ. He looks back and sees God's hand leading him into the mediation profession as a precursor to writing his PLAY NICE in Your Sandbox book series.

Ron resides in Farmington, New Mexico, with his wife Maridell (40 years and counting) and their menagerie of cats and one dog. He enjoys, among other pursuits, Crossword puzzles, Cryptoquotes, Disc Golf, Pickleball, and Tennis.

As an Advanced Toastmaster Silver, and current member of the National Speakers Association, Ron loves to entertain audiences while he gives them practical information they can incorporate into their lives to enhance their relationships at work, home, and the church.

To contact Ron, you may call him at 505 324-6328,

or

send an email to Ron@PlayNiceinYourSandbox.com,

or

connect with him on Linked In at

https://www.linkedin.com/in/ronpriceproductiveoutcomes/

or

Facebook at https://www.facebook.com/Productiveoutcomes/

or
subscribe to his Ron Price You Tube Channel. There is more than one
Ron Price so be sure to pick the best looking one ☺

Printed in the USA
CPSIA information can be obtained
at www.ICGtesting.com
JSHW022339140824
68134JS00019B/1580